Olga Shmatova

Techniques
Gouache Painting
for Beginners

vol.2

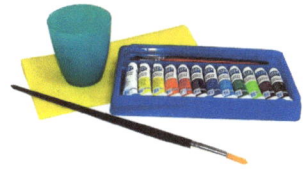

2010

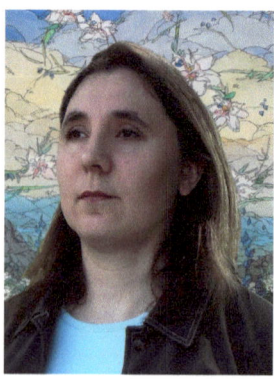

Gouache

Gouache colors are popular with many designers, but they can used also for painting.

Rich choice of colors and easy mixing, quick drying and easy correcting, odorless and does not require bulky equipment. All this are made gouache an excellent choice for beginner painter. Work in gouache can be easily switch to other paint: oil or acrylic.

Olga Shmatova

Techniques Gouache Painting for Beginners vol.2
Olga Shmatova

The author thanks for providing pictures of his students:

Galina Kulikova
Naila Alyautdinova
Marina Kurdyukova
Svetlana Sapozhnikova
Andrew Shishov
Natalia Sudakova
Tatiana Veselova
Valentina Gritsenko
Julia Afonina
Galina Solovieva
Eugene Neroznikova
Nina Kulikova
Maria Bogdanova
Anastasia Seryabryakova

idea, text, schemes, illustrations and design by Olga Shmatova

photos by Sergey Kuzmichev
translate by Sergey Kuzmichev

This is third publication (fully modification) 2010 year
First publication 2005 year by EKSMO, Moskow

error

picture by beginner painter

Table of Content

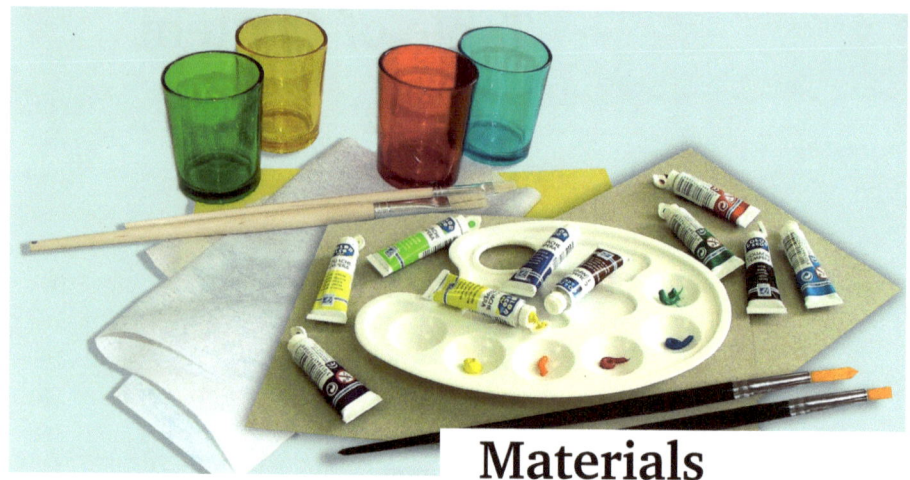

Materials

For employment are needed:

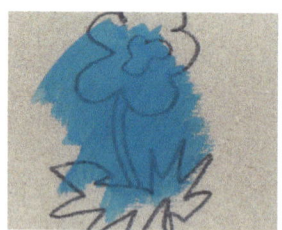

Very liquid paint.

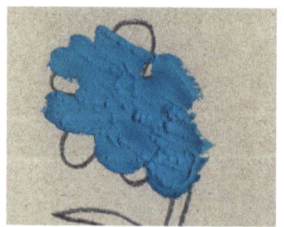

Very thick paint.

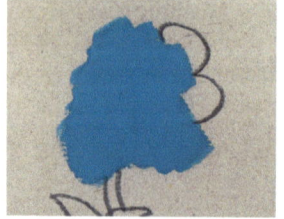

The paint is normal consistency.

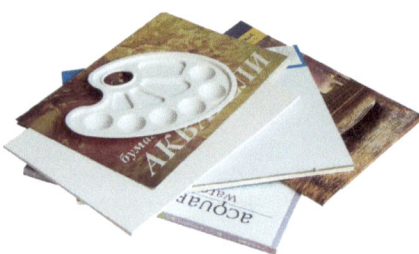

The plastic palette.

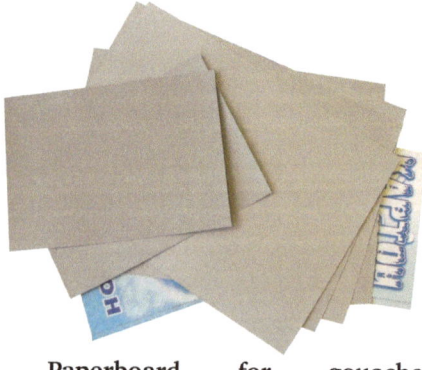

Paperboard for gouache painting.

Paint

Gouache set of 12 colors.

Brushes

Syntetic round brush No 7
Syntetic round brush No 1
Syntetic flat brush No 4.

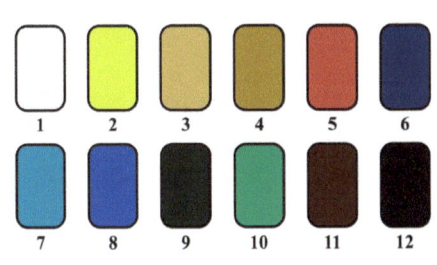

Gouache set of 12 colors.

Support

A few sheets of paperboard 20x30 sm (8x12 in), 200 g/m2 (53 lb) or thicker. Sheet will.

For drawing

Pencil 3b and eraser.

Tablet

The tablet is used as hard support for sheets. Tablets are made of plywood or hardboard. The area of your tablet should be larger then the area of sheet.

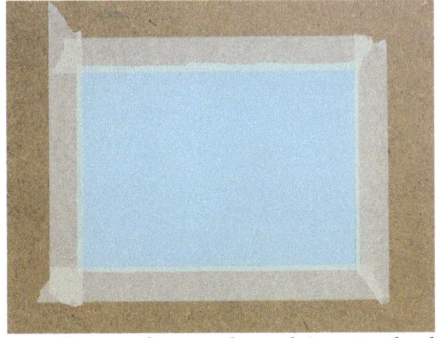

Sheet of paperboard is attached to tablet with paper tape.

Paper adhesive tape

Sheets is attached to the tablet with paper adhesive tape.

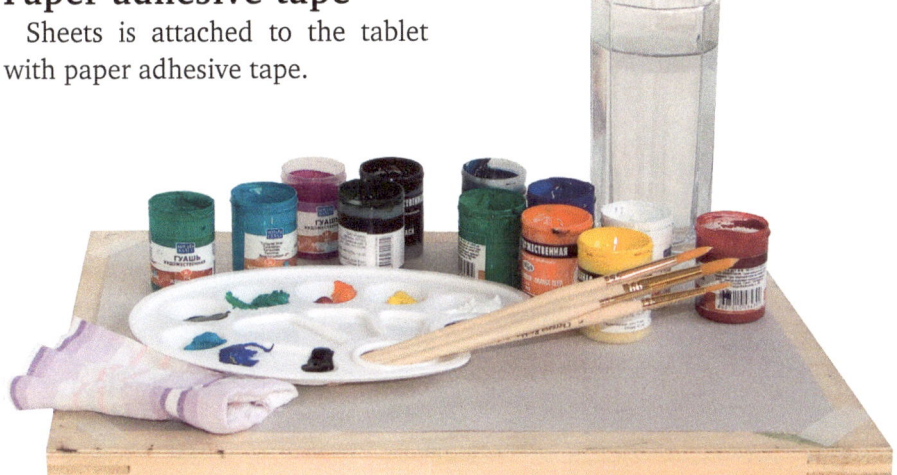

Painting equipment.

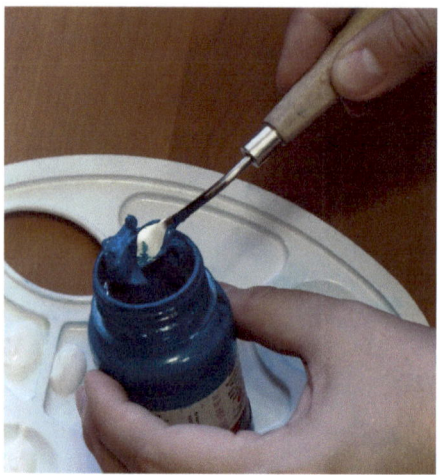

The paint is convenient taking out from jar with painting knife.

Palette

The palette is used for paint and color mixing. For gouache is used plastic palettes. The palette should be white. In an extreme case it may be replaced disposable plate. More convenient to use two or three palettes.

Jar of water

Water is used for washing brushes and dilution paint. Jar should be no less 200 ml (6 oz).

Rag for brushes

Brushes are wiped with a rag. If do otherwise, then water will be transfered on palette with brush. Over time paint on palette will be very liquid.

Painting knife

Painting knife is used to move a paint on the palette from jar. If your used paint tubes, then painting knife not needed.

The jars of paint should be open in work time.

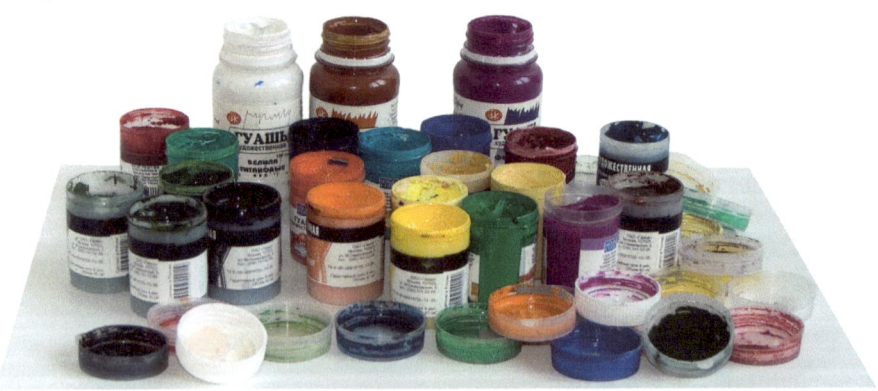

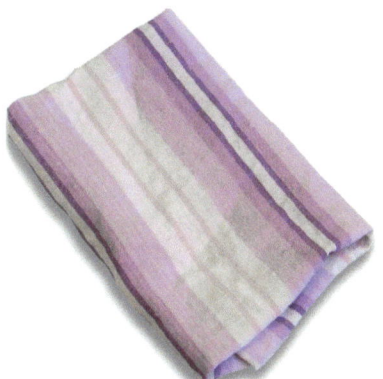

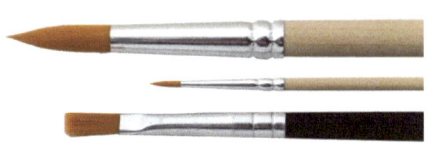

The syntetic round brush No 7, syntetic round brush No 1 and syntetic flat brush No 4.

The rag for wiping brushes.

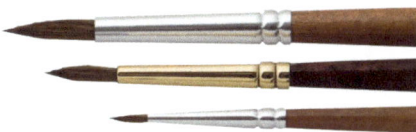

The sable brush can used for gouache painting.

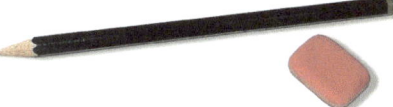

The simple pencil and eraser.

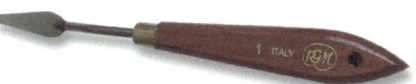

The painting knife.

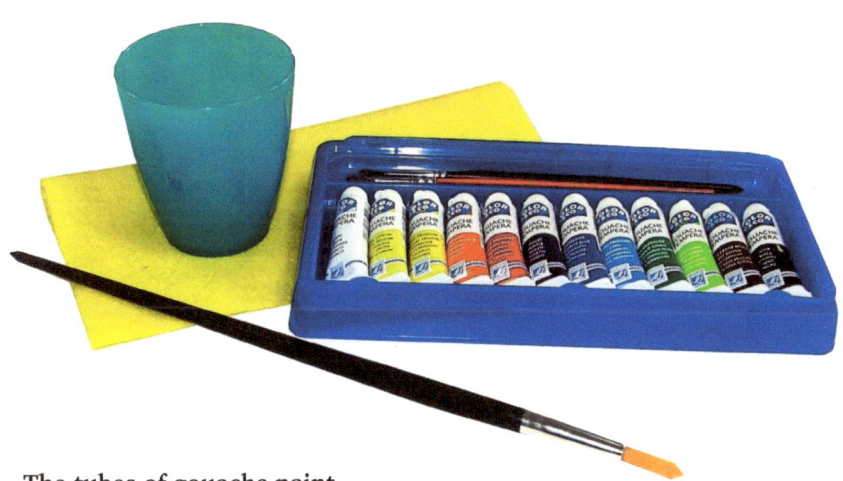

The tubes of gouache paint.

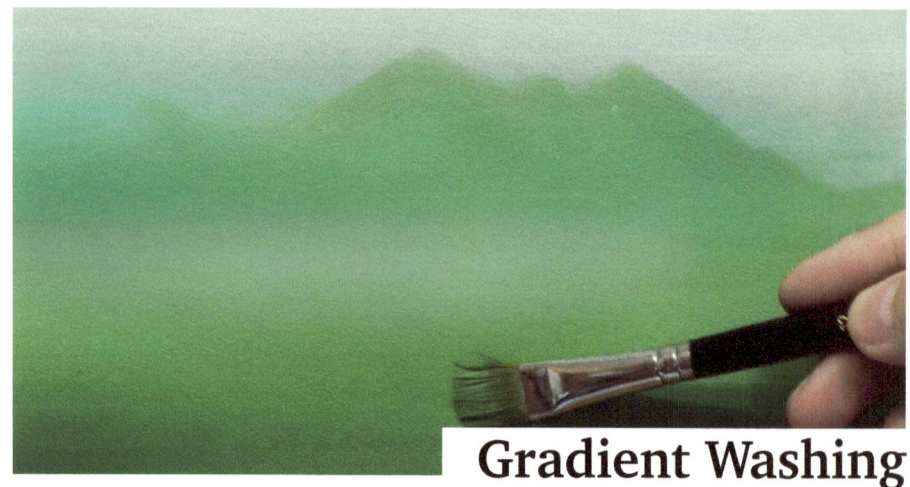

Gradient Washing

Popularity: 3 from 5

Color gradient to large area is making with technique gradient washing.

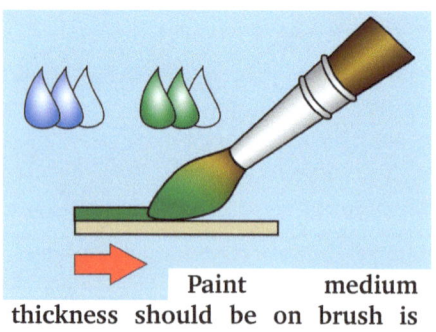

Paint medium thickness should be on brush is not very much. A sheet begin paint from the top edge is gradually moving down.

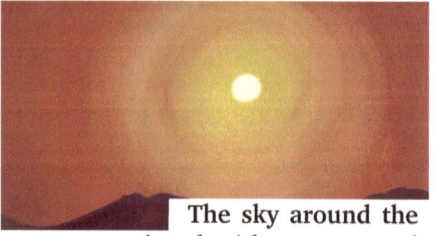

The sky around the sun was painted with use a round wash. The sun was painted with technique a opaque layers.

The gradient washing is easy and effective technique. Moutains, sky, water and other like them, makes illusion of space are made with this technique.

Gouache pictures were made with gradient washing are quite spectacular.

Such pictures are quite spectacular.

Effect of gradient washing in gouache like washing in watercolor.

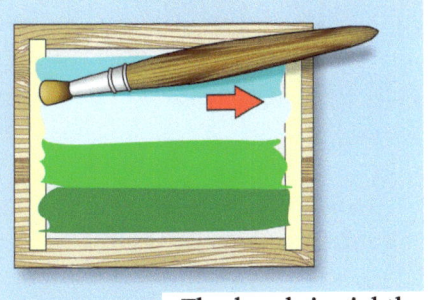

The brush is rightly moved forward shaft.

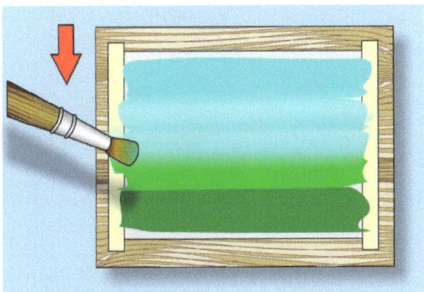

The brush is stopped on edges of sheet. In stop point the brush is lifted and after this it is moved in opposite direction.

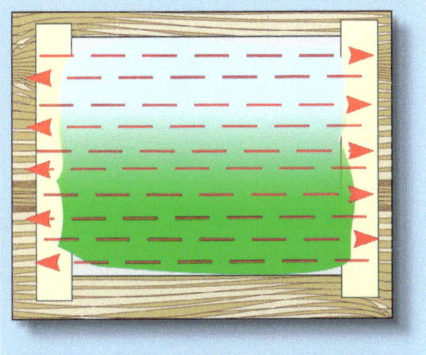

The edges of colors bands applying in first stage are blended with a lot of brush stroke.

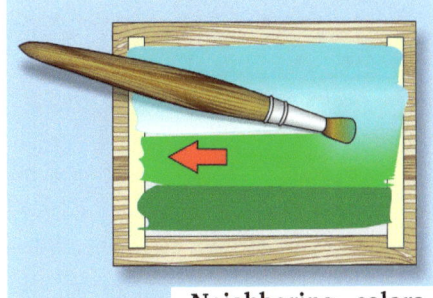

Neighboring colors were blended with a lot of brush stroke.

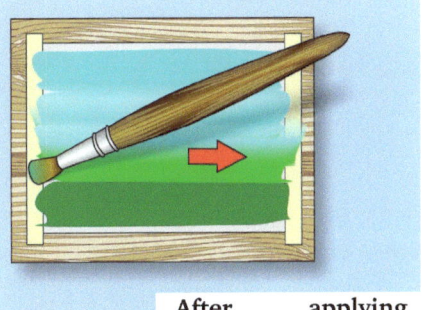

After applying band: the brush is shifted on third down.

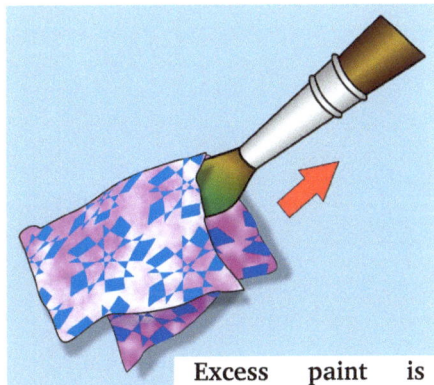

Excess paint is removed from a brush with water and after this the brush is wiped with rag.

Stages of Technique

1. A sheet of paperboard is attached to tablet on the left and right sides with a paper adhesive tape.

2. Color mixtures are made on palette. The good effect will be if colors of mixtures will be very different. The paint should be moderate thickness, but not be very liquid. Sufficiently consistency like liquid sour cream.

3. The entire sheet is painted with bands of color mixtures. If two bands: first - from the top to the middle, second - from the middle (bottom edge of first band) to the bottom edge of the sheet. Area of sheet is painted without gaps. Paint should be apply quickly, to it did not have time dry.

4. From an angle of top edges of sheet: wet paint is spread with a brush with color mixture of top color band. The brush is moved forward shaft. On the brush strong pressures, so that the its hair from tip to base of brush touches the sheet.

The brush is stopped on tape. In stop point the brush is lifted, it is shifted on third down, after this: on it is strong pressed and moved in opposite direction.

The brush is not rotated.

This is being repeated, until the brush is not reaching bottom edge of sheet.

5. When the brush is reaching bottom edge of sheet. The previous step is made again, but the brush is lifted and it is shifted up on a third . And this is being repeated, until the brush is not reaching upper edge of sheet.

The brush is not washed.

6. Two previous steps are being done, until borders between color bands will not be blurred.

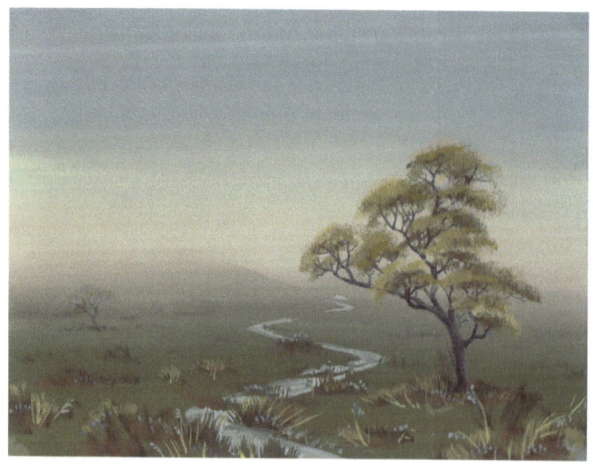

The work by professional painter. Sky, hills and ground were painted with wash.

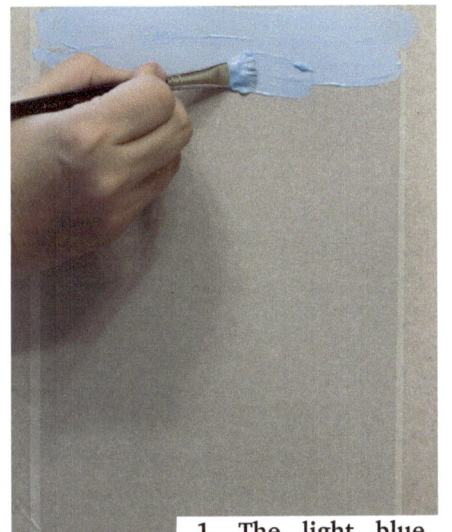

1. The light blue band is applied on sheet.

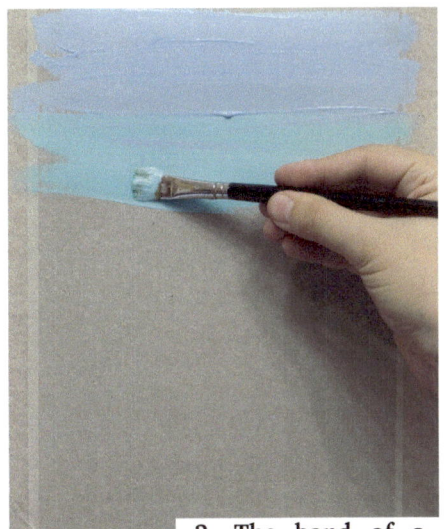

2. The band of a other blue shade is applied on sheet. Paint of this band and paint of the previous band are not mixed.

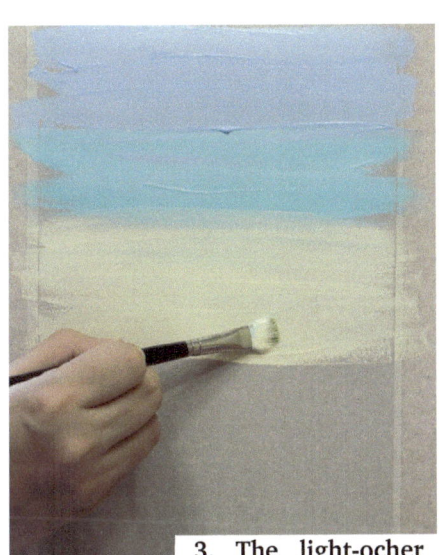

3. The light-ocher band is applied on sheet. Gaps should not be.

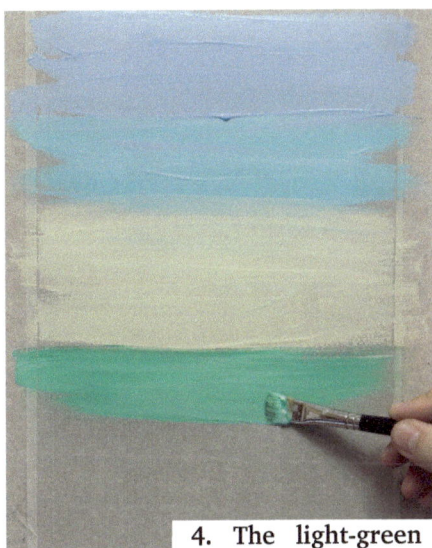

4. The light-green band is applied on sheet. This should do quickly, to paint did not have time dry.

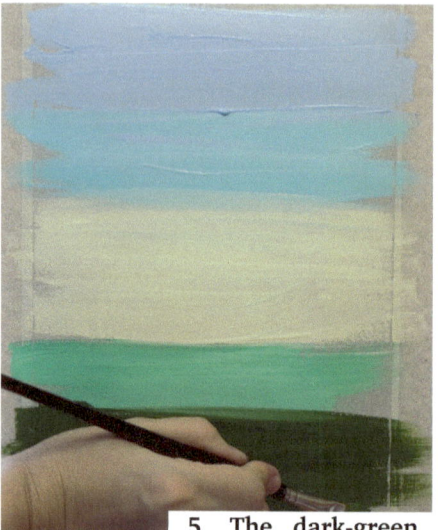

5. The dark-green band is applied on sheet.

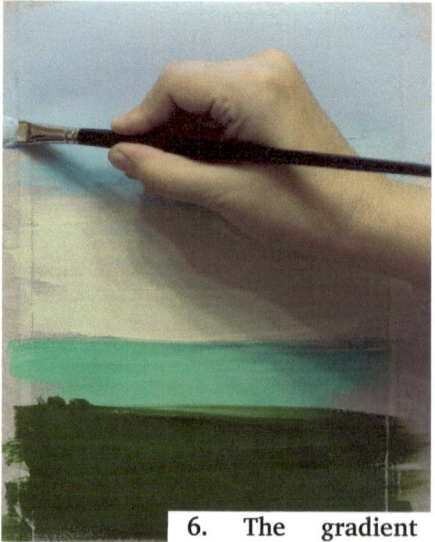

6. The gradient washing is started from upper band. The brush is wetted to color mixture of upper band.

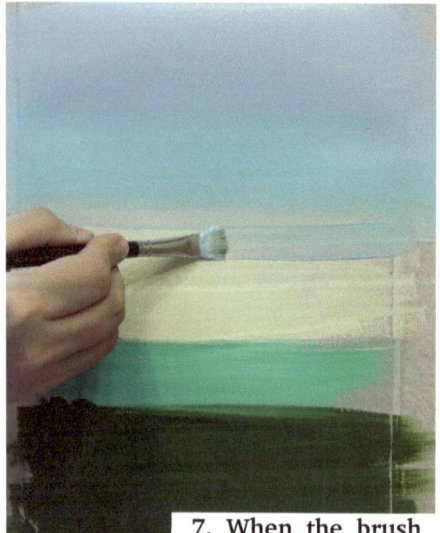

7. When the brush reaches the light-ocher band, it is moved without stop.

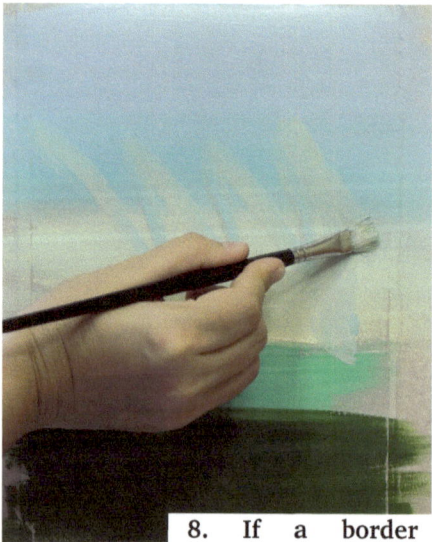

8. If a border between color bands are visible, they can be blended with zig-zag movements. After this wash is doing again.

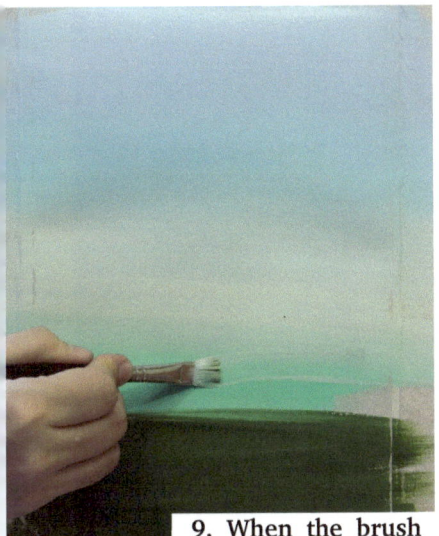

9. When the brush reaches the light-green band, it is moved without stop.

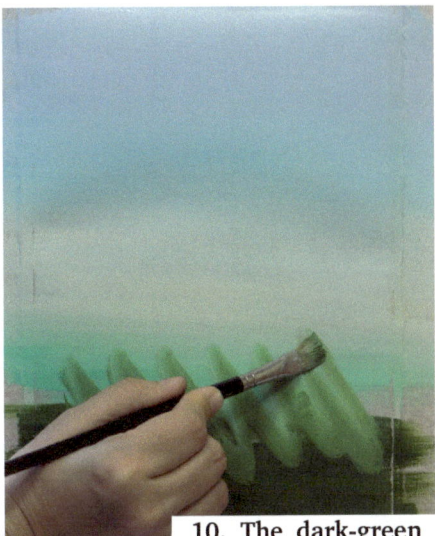

10. The dark-green color was spread with zig-zag movements.

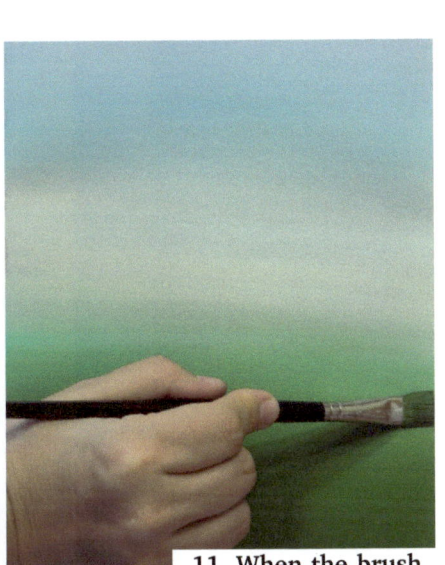

11. When the brush reaches bottom edge of gradient washing, it is not stopping. The wash is done but from bottom up.

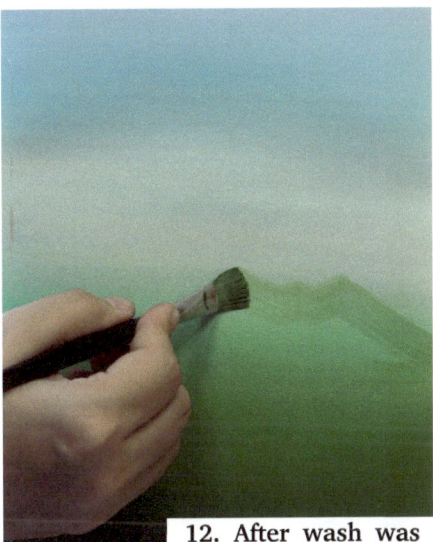

12. After wash was spread from bottom up, the green band was moved up. On wet gradient washing is applied added details. The contour of hill was painted with an unwashed brush.

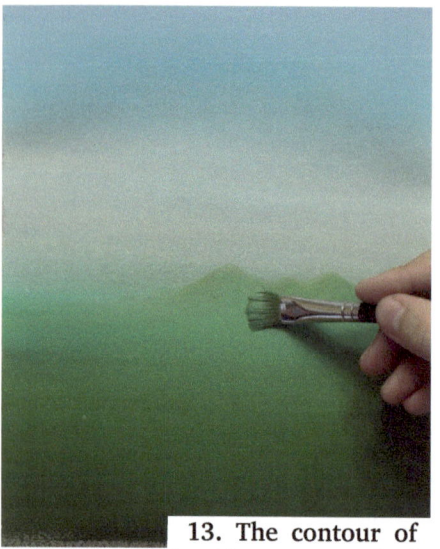

13. The contour of hill was filled with an unwashed brush.

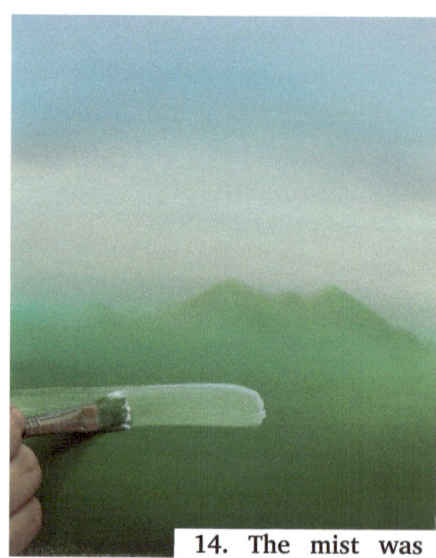

14. The mist was painted with a gouache on wet wash.

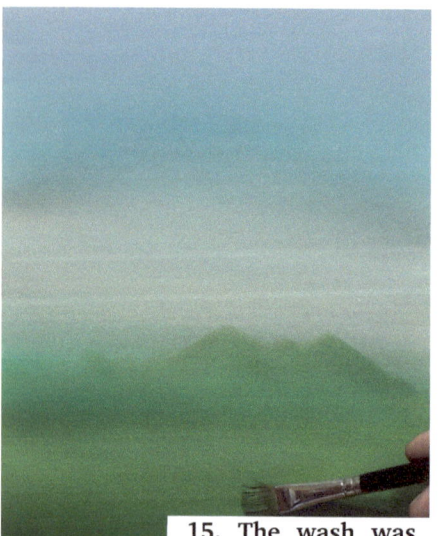

15. The wash was spread to bottom, and after to up, to the foot of the hill.

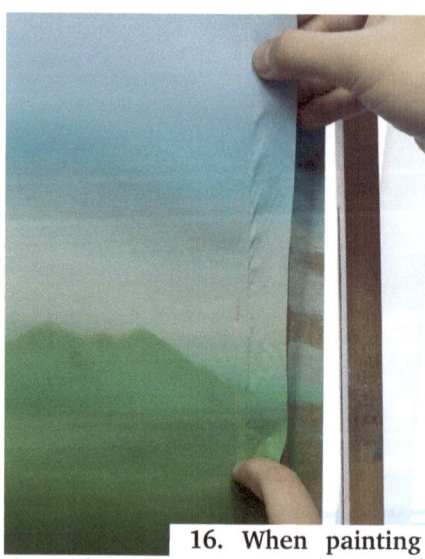

16. When painting is ready, it is separated from tape.

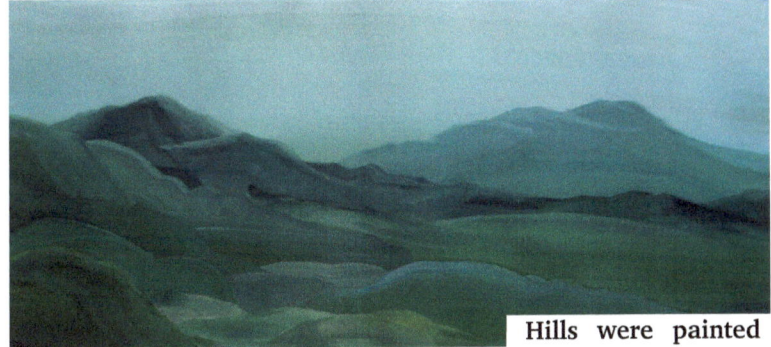

Hills were painted on wet gradient wash.

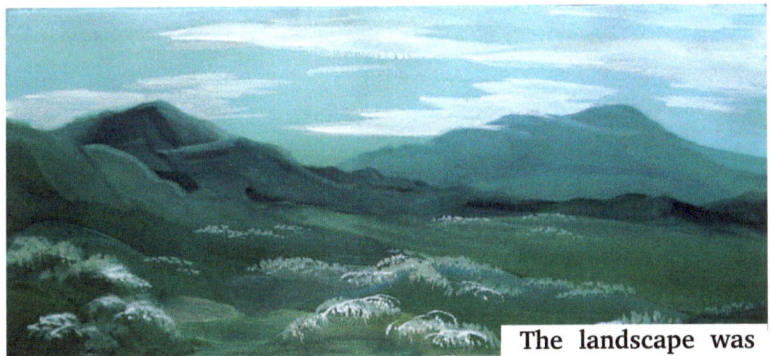

The landscape was painted on base wash with hills.

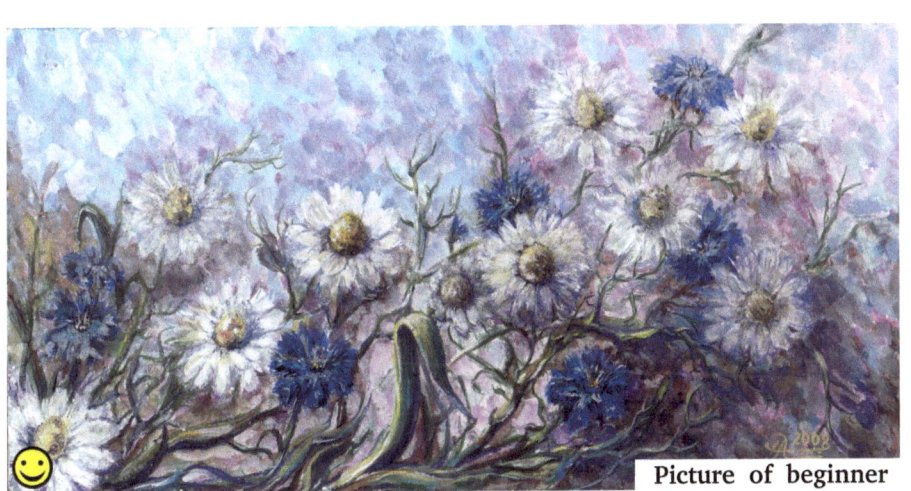

Picture of beginner painter. The picture was made with brushstrokes on base of wash.

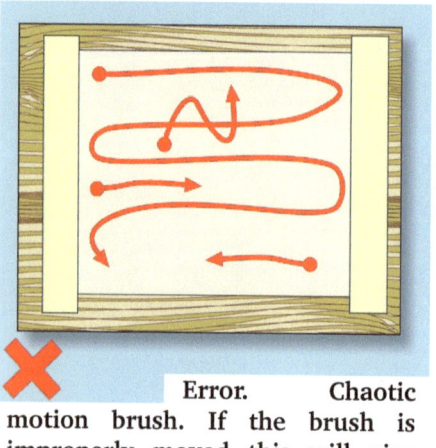

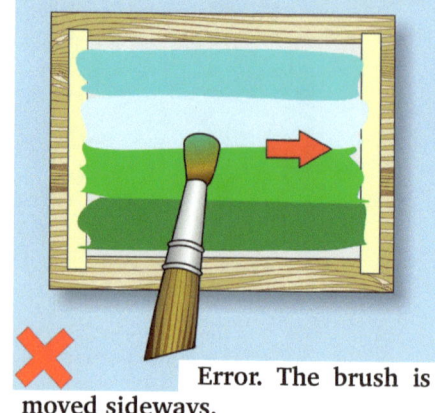

Error. Chaotic motion brush. If the brush is improperly moved this will give stains and drips.

Error. The brush is moved sideways.

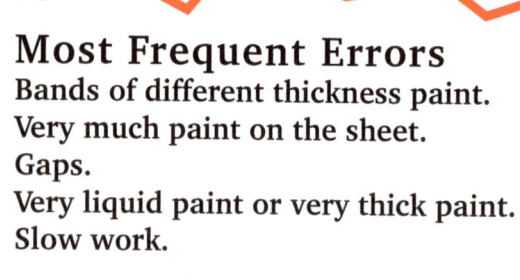

Most Frequent Errors
Bands of different thickness paint.
Very much paint on the sheet.
Gaps.
Very liquid paint or very thick paint.
Slow work.

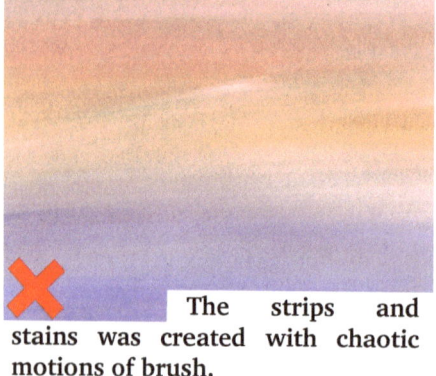

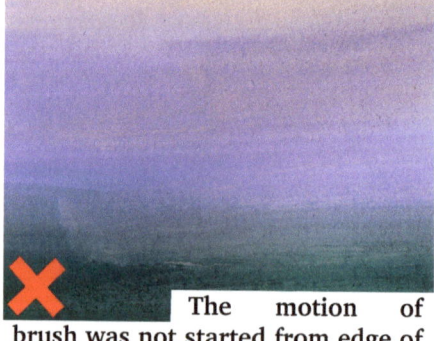

The strips and stains was created with chaotic motions of brush.

The motion of brush was not started from edge of sheet.

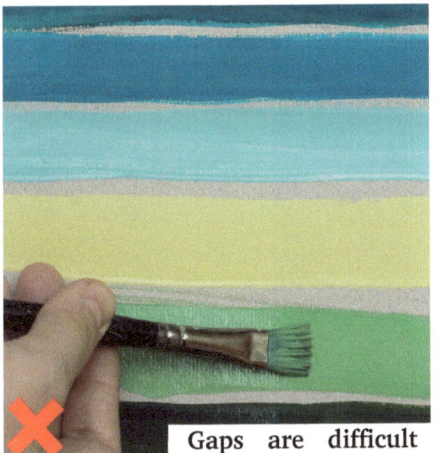

Gaps are difficult making a wash.

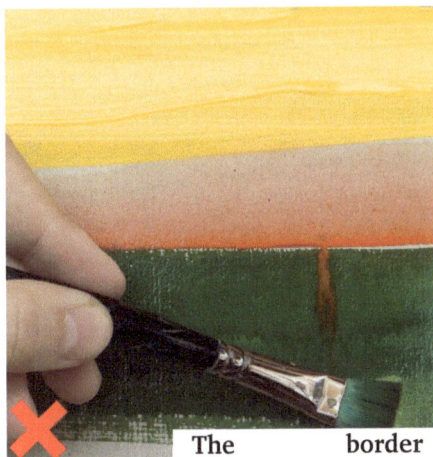

The border between color bands poorly blurred. Color bands dry at different rates.

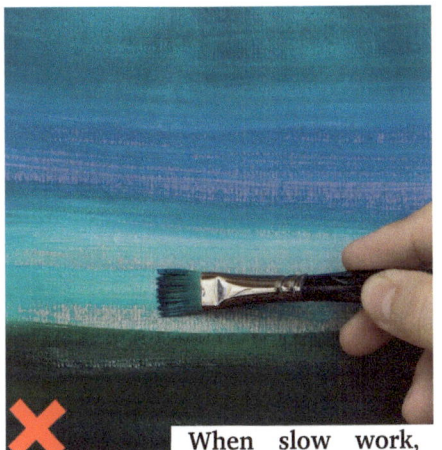

When slow work, paint will dry and will instead wash will effect of dry brushwork.

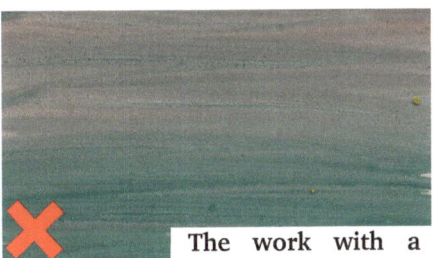

The work with a brush point.

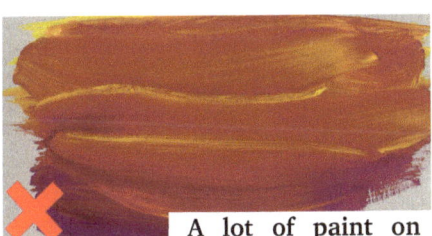

A lot of paint on brush.

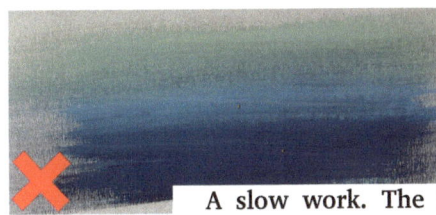

A slow work. The paint was dried before complete wash.

Exercises

Color Bands

Take sheet of paperboard 10x10 cm (4x4 in). Make on this sheet washes:

Dark-blue and light-blue
Dark-green and light yellow-green
Ocher and light-yellow
White and black
Light-pink and dark-blue
Light-blue and brown
Light-blue, blue and black
Red, pink and yellow
Light-blue, ocher and dark-green

Different Liquid

Make washes with more liquid paint and with more thick paint. Pay attention: a wash is made with a thick paint different with different ease.

Four Color Wash

Make a wash from any four colors and/or color mixtures.

Several Washes

Make several washes. The border between color bands should be less smooth. If bands will be at an angle or there borders will be uneven, then gradient washing will like mountainscape or seascape.

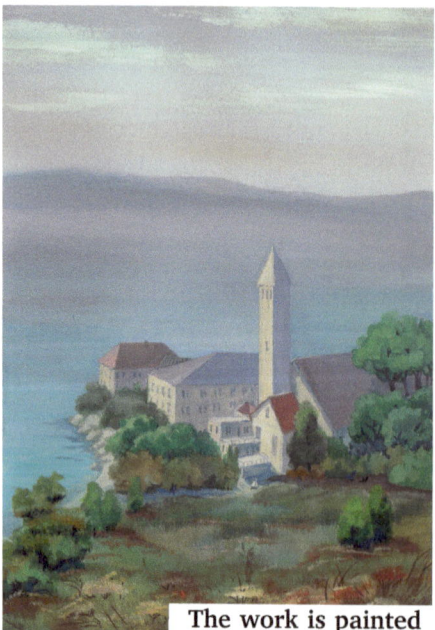

The work is painted in base wash and with use: uniform staining, blurred brushstrokes, dry brushwork, softening edges and gouache liquid first layer.

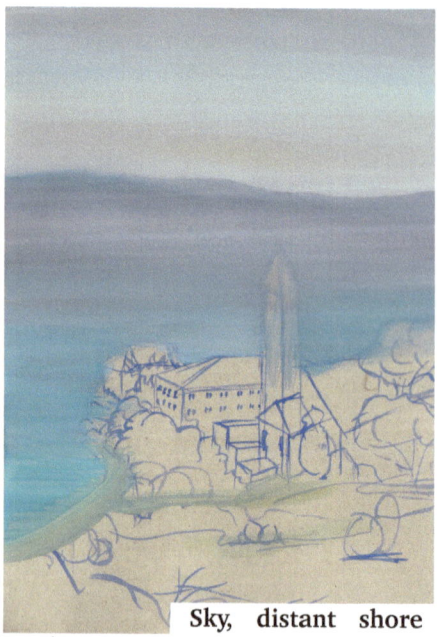

Sky, distant shore and sea were painted with wash.

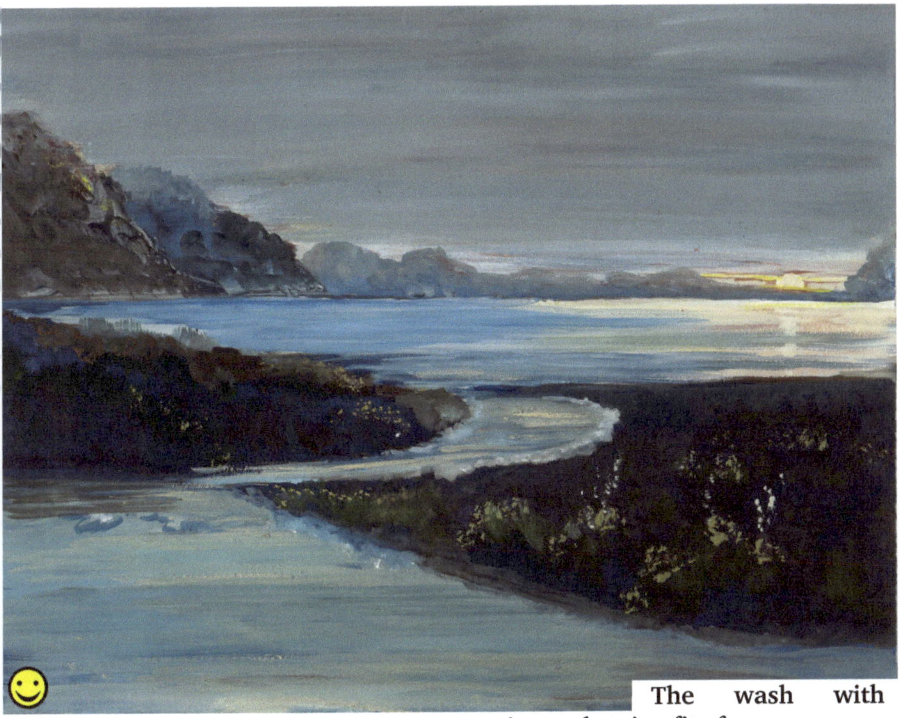

The wash with strips and stains fits for seascape.

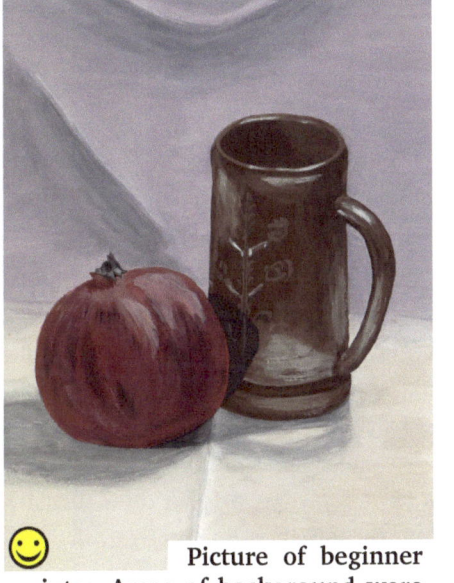

Picture of beginner painter. Areas of background were painted with wash. Folds were painted with gouache liquid.

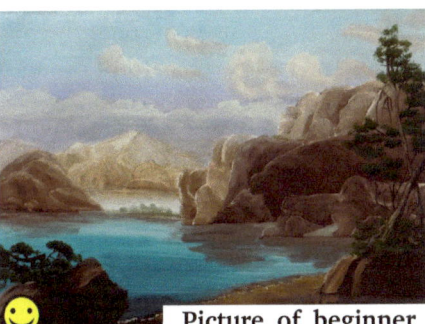

Picture of beginner painter. Sky and water were made with use technique wash.

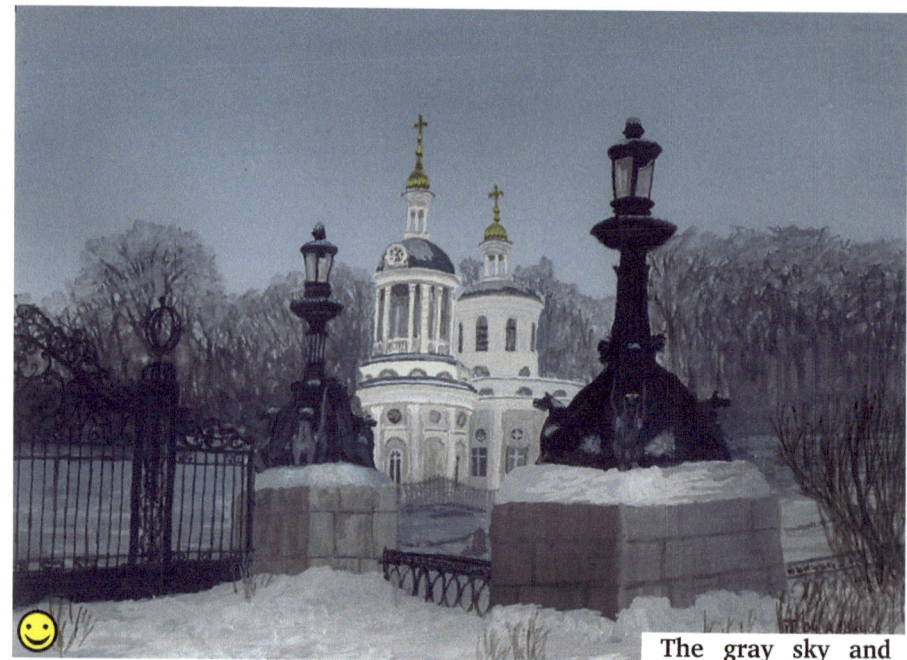

The gray sky and low layer of forest were painted with wash.

Helpful Tips

A wet thin sheet of paperboard when dry is may curl up into a tube. For ease paint it is attached to tablet with pushpins or paper adhesive tape.

A wash should be on a all area of sheet. If tablet will be sullied do not worry. Its done for this.

The brush is moved forward shaft and its trace like snail trace.

If paint dried before complete wash. Wait complete drying of wash. When paint will dry it is carefully (otherwise paint layer will be dissolved) wetted with clear water. On surface should not be puddles. Wet wash is continued painted as usual.

If all colors of wash are mixed to one color – stopping! The common cause of a mixing colors: lot of paint on sheet or improper brush. If paint on brush like lump a such brush should replace.

In case of difficulties of wash, take a small sheet or a other brush. On a small sheet easily to train.

The large wash is made with a large brush. The small wash is made with a small brush.

Compatibility with Other Techniques

Gradient washing can be used together with any techniques, except: liquid gouache.

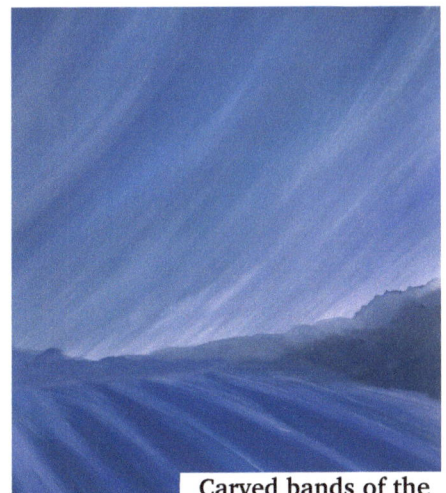

Carved bands of the wash were painted at an angle.

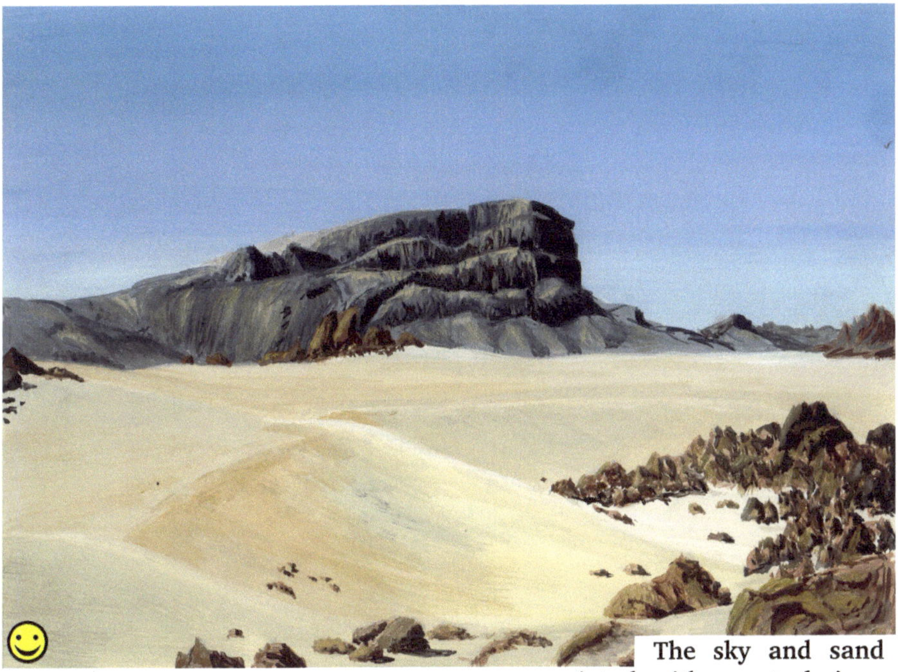

The sky and sand were painted with use technique wash. The mount, stones and details of dunes were painted with opaque layer, brushstrokes, wash paint and wash water.

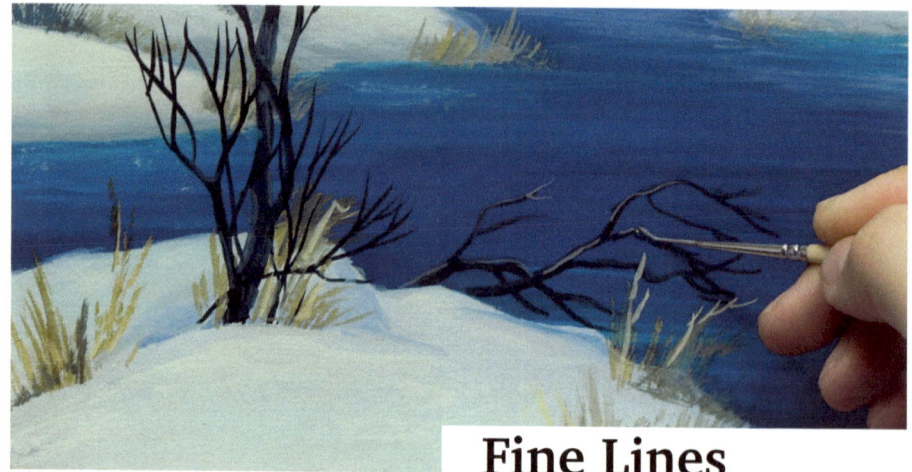

Fine Lines

Popularity: 3 from 5

This technique used for painting fine lines with gouache.

The beginner painter in gouache have often difficult paint fine lines with a brush. A small experience is cause uneven lines, mistakes of place of brushstrokes and brush point, and in fine details.

A rightly brushwork simplifies to painting fine lines.

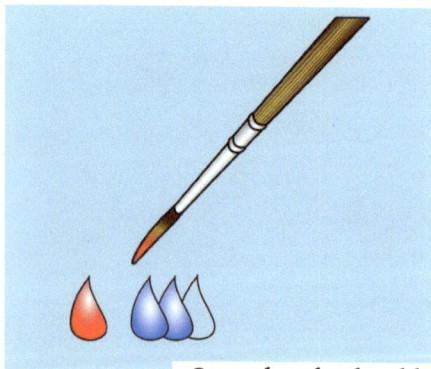

On a brush should not be a lot of paint.

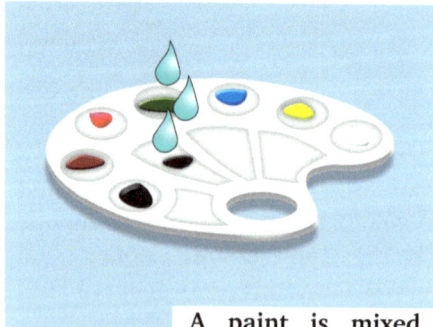

A paint is mixed with a lot of water on palette.

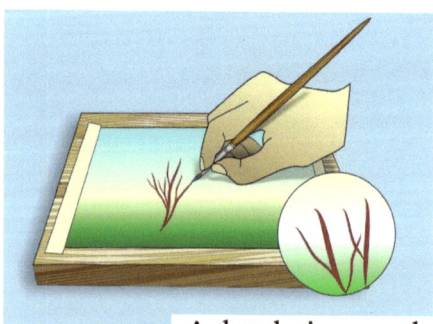

A brush is moved an acute angle to sheet and is not hight lifted above the surface of sheet.

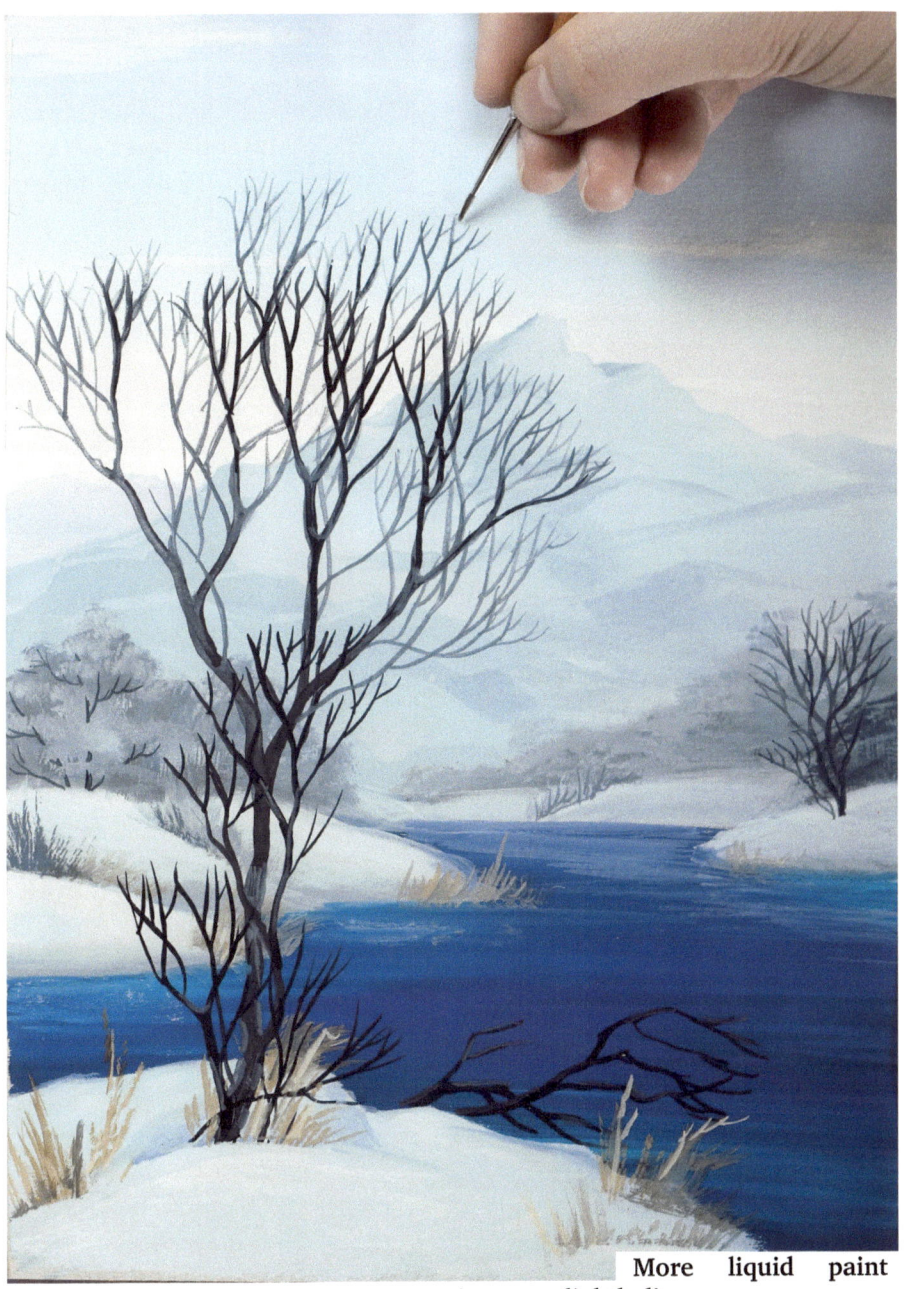

More liquid paint give more lightly lines.

Wide branches were painted with a thin brush too. Lines were painted twice or new line was painted to parallel previous.

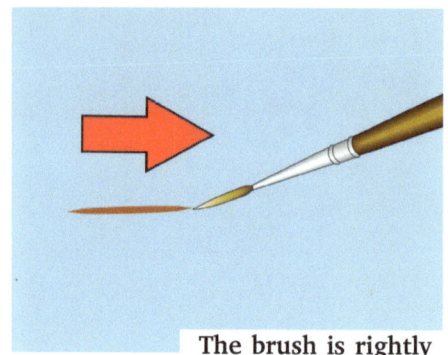

The brush is rightly moved forward shaft.

Stages of Technique

1. A paint is thoroughly mixed with a lot of water on palette.

2. A thin round brush is dipped into paint and tested on draft.

If a lot of paint on the brush, its trace will be wide and may be puddles. The brush is wiped with rag and dipped again.

If a little paint on the brush, its trace will have gaps. The brush is dipped again.

3. The brush is moved forward shaft, like boat is towed with hand. Its trace lefts after this, like trace of boat.

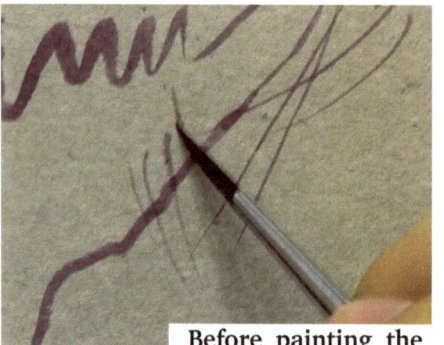

Before painting the paint is checked on draft.

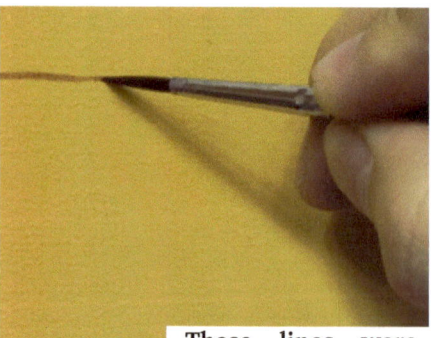

These lines were painted rightly.

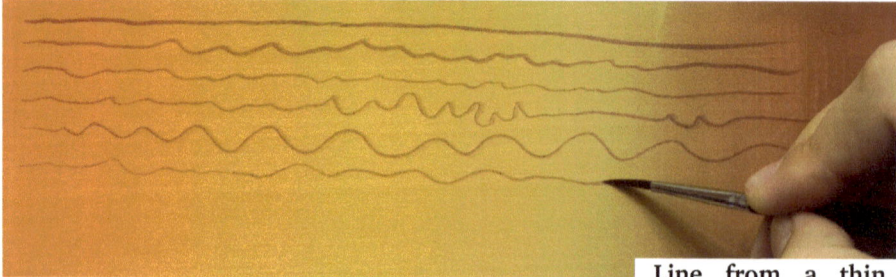

Line from a thin brush (dipped one time) can be longer than 1 m (3 ft).

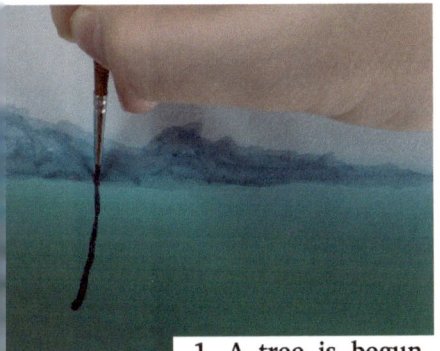

1. A tree is begun painted from shaft, as it grow: from root and up.

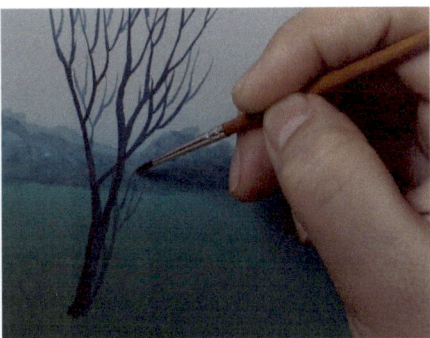

2. Branches are painted from shaft to tips.

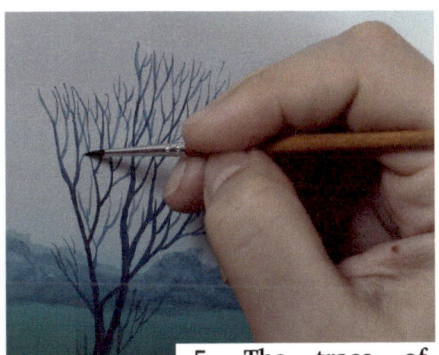

3. A paint ends and trace of brush becomes lighter. Small branches look more natural.

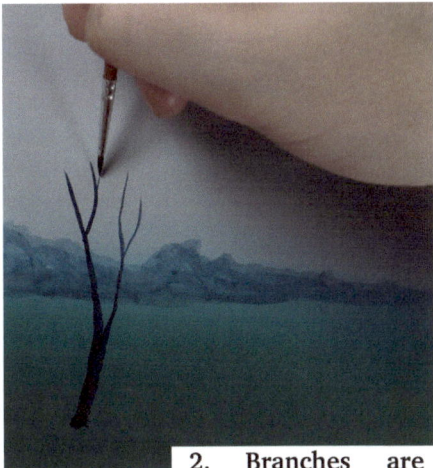

4. The hand is closer to brush's hair, the more aligned strips.

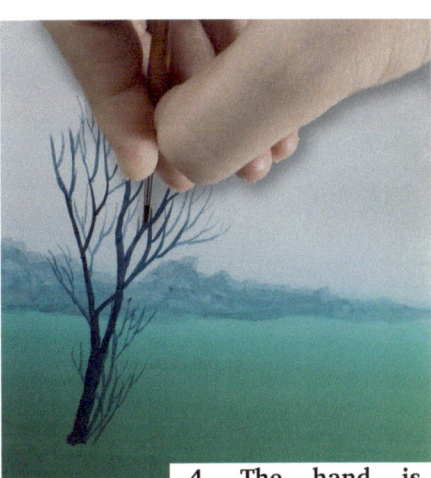

5. The trace of brush may be uneven. Need change of hand's position or change position of sheet.

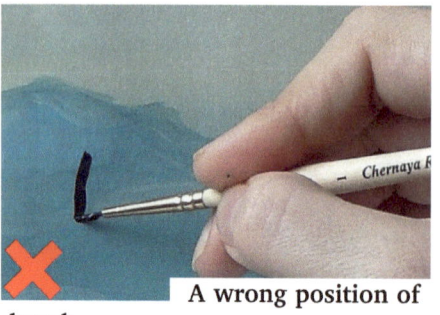

❌ A wrong position of brush.

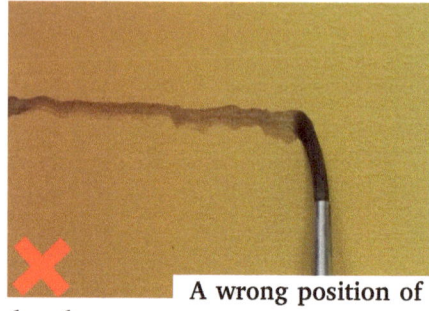

❌ A wrong position of brush.

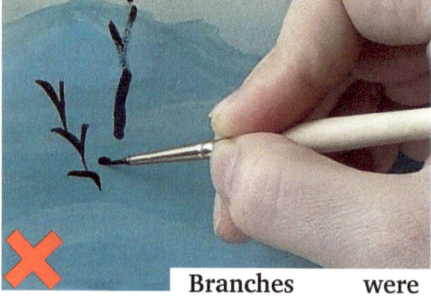

❌ Branches were begun painted from tips to shaft.

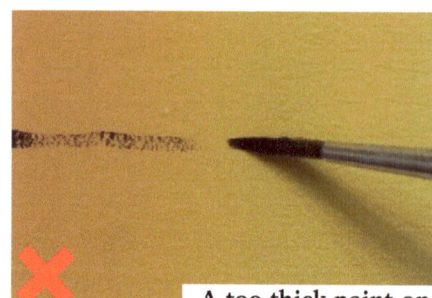

❌ A too thick paint on the brush.

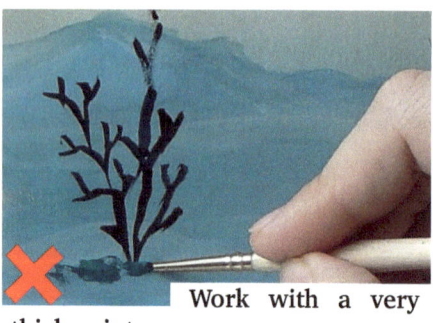

❌ Work with a very thick paint.

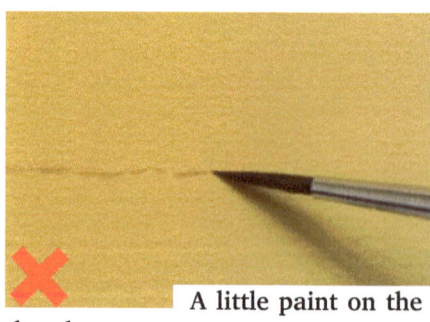

❌ A little paint on the brush.

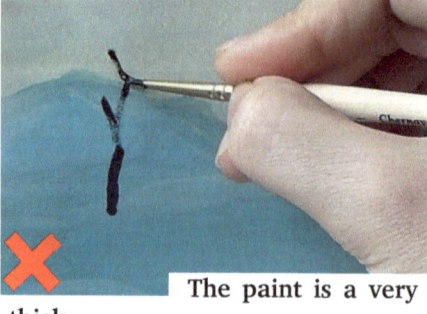

❌ The paint is a very thick.

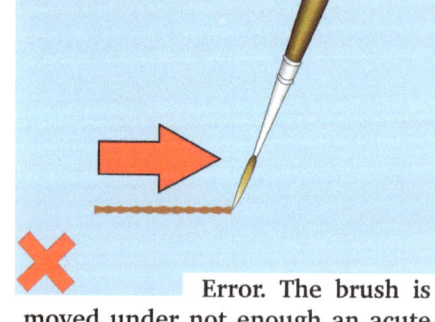

❌ Error. The brush is moved under not enough an acute angle to sheet.

Most Frequent Errors

Thick paint on the brush.

Little paint on the brush.

A fine line is painted with a brush is held onto a far end of shaft.

A fine line is painted with a hand without support.

A brush is not tested on draft.

A line is not painted with a brush point.

A wrong position of brush.

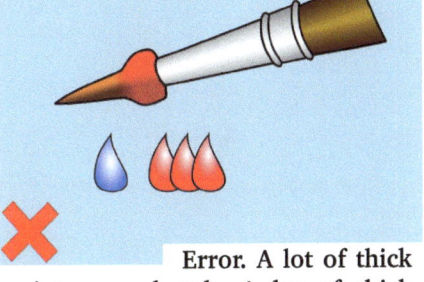

Error. A lot of thick paint on a brush. A lot of thick paint on a brush. A thick paint moved from brush point near base of the brush's hair.

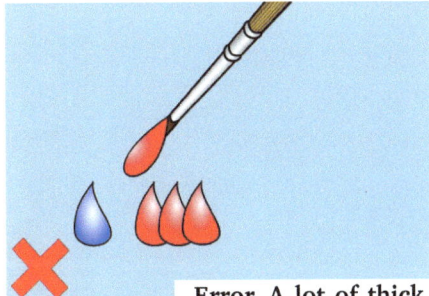

Error. A lot of thick paint on a brush.

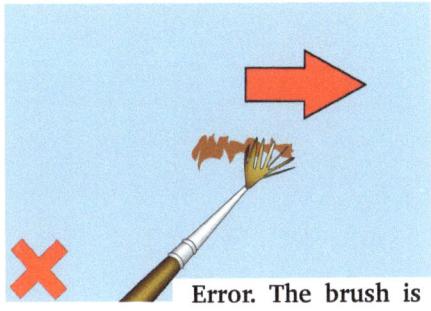

Error. The brush is moved forward hair.

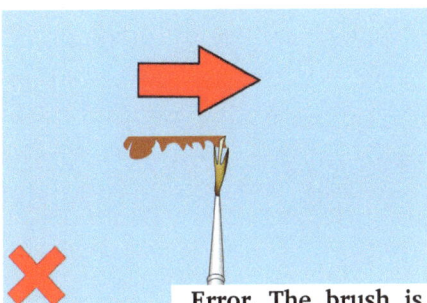

Error. The brush is moved sideways.

Exercises

Elementary Exercise
Take ready gradient washing. Draw lines on gradient washing with a hard pencil. Paint lines with a thin brush along these lines.

The Trees
Take ready gradient washing with light top and dark bottom. Paint with a thin brush on this wash a thin tree without leaves. Paint near this tree a few trees like this.

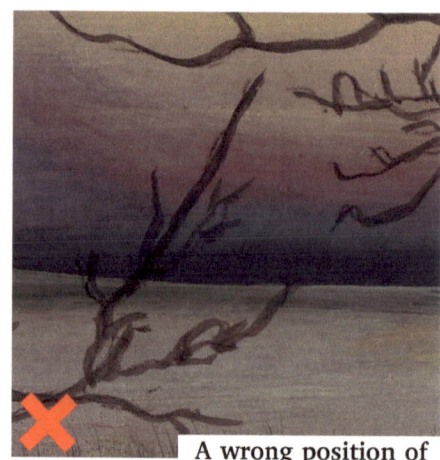

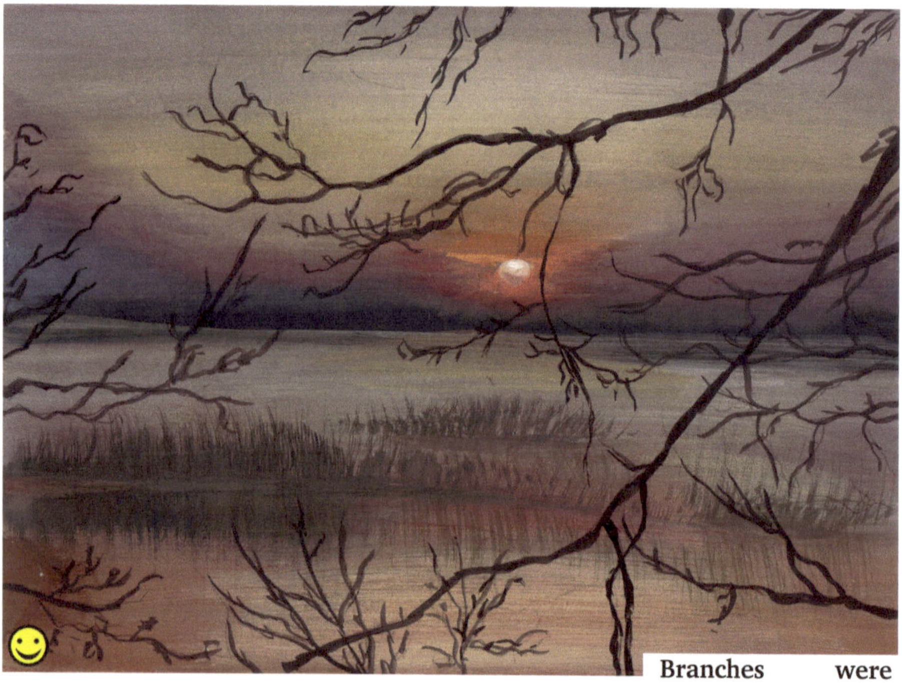

A wrong position of brush.

Branches were painted with fine lines, but an wrong angle, therefore lines with gaps. A few branches were painted thick paint.

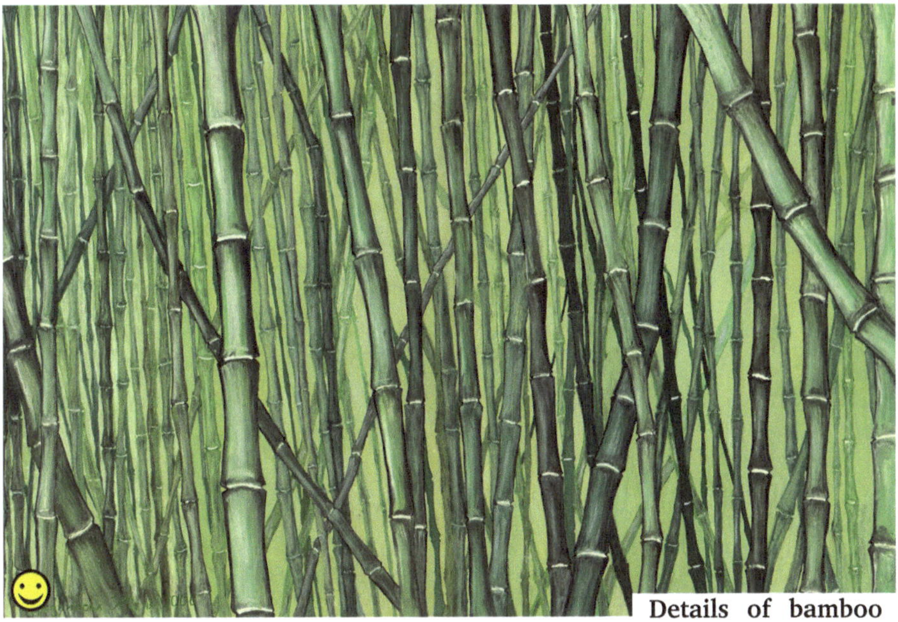

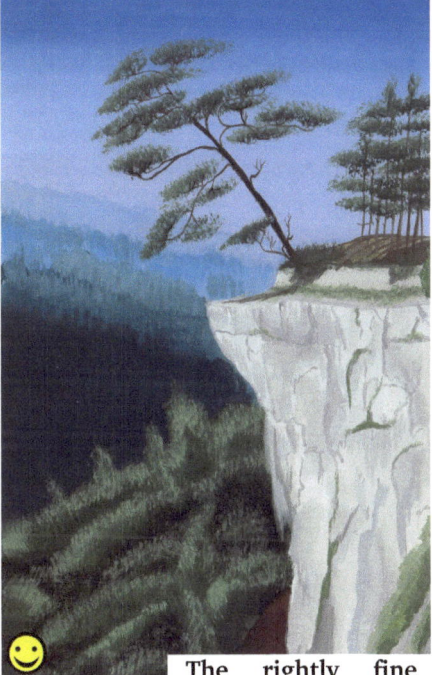

Details of bamboo were painted with technique fine lines.

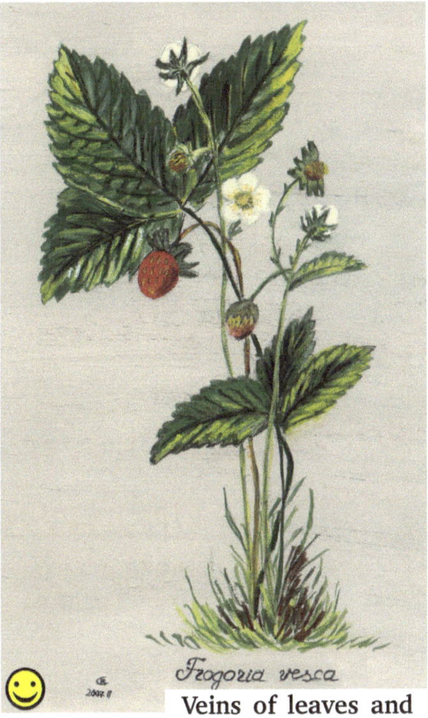

Veins of leaves and other details were painted with technique fine lines.

The rightly fine lines.

Helpful Tips

Fine line is painted only brush point. Base paintbrush is not touched sheet.

The hand is closer to brush's hair, the more aligned strips.

A brush is moved an acute angle to sheet and is not hight lifted above the surface of sheet.

For very good result of painting fine lines you need experience. You can train on a lined paper. The paper can be line with pencil. But better if you will train on ready gradient washings. But better if you will train on ready gradient washings. This is closer to real work, and given notion of as gouache will lay down on gouache.

Fine details are painted without support is difficult. For your ease you can put your hand on sheet of paperboard. A paper sheet is put under hand. This saves gouache of damage.

Please, position sheet as more convenient for you.

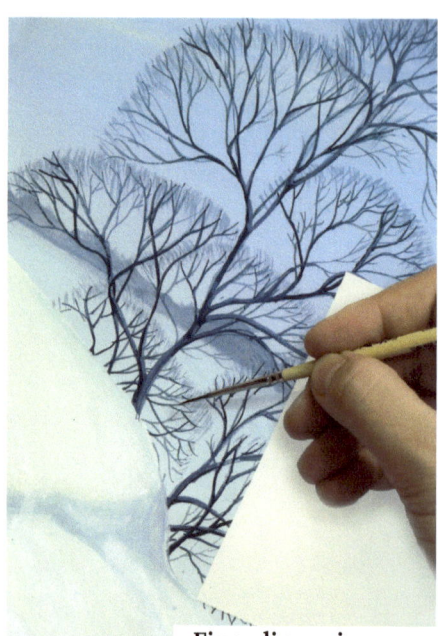

Fine lines is easy painted if hand is put on sheet. For ease of work you can rotate sheet.

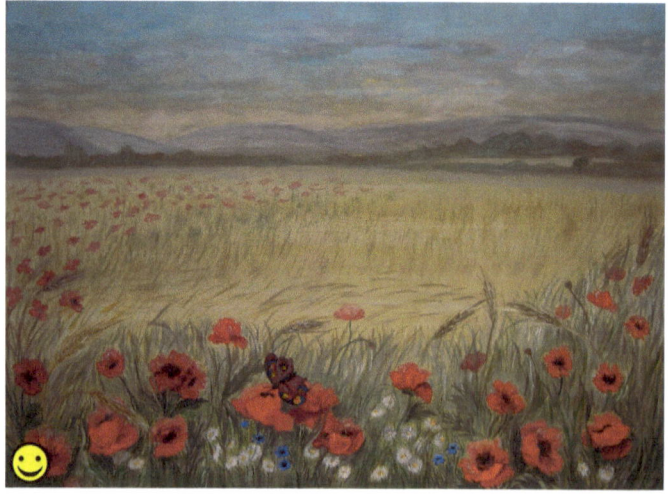

Distant grass were painted with a dry brushwork, and nearby grass were painted with a fine lines.

Compatibility with Other Techniques

The fine lines can be used together with any techniques, except: sharp and multicolors brushstrokes, blurred brushstrokes.

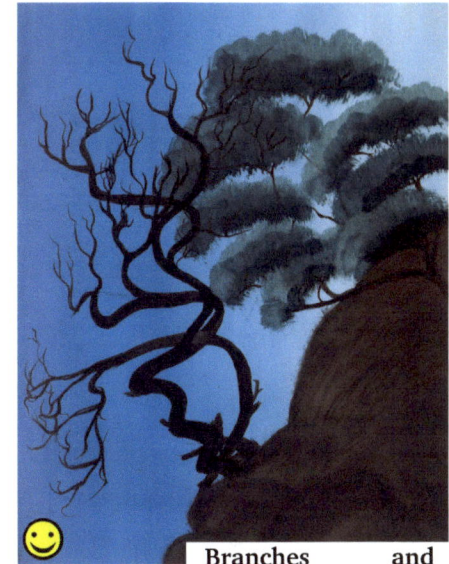

Branches and shafts of trees were painted with fine lines.

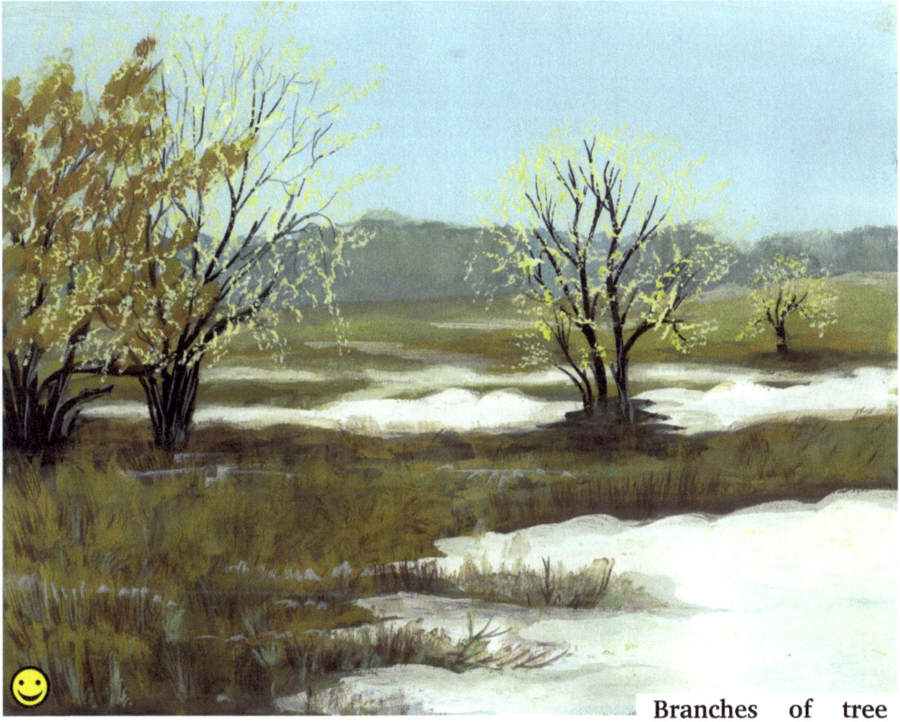

Branches of tree were painted with technique fine lines.

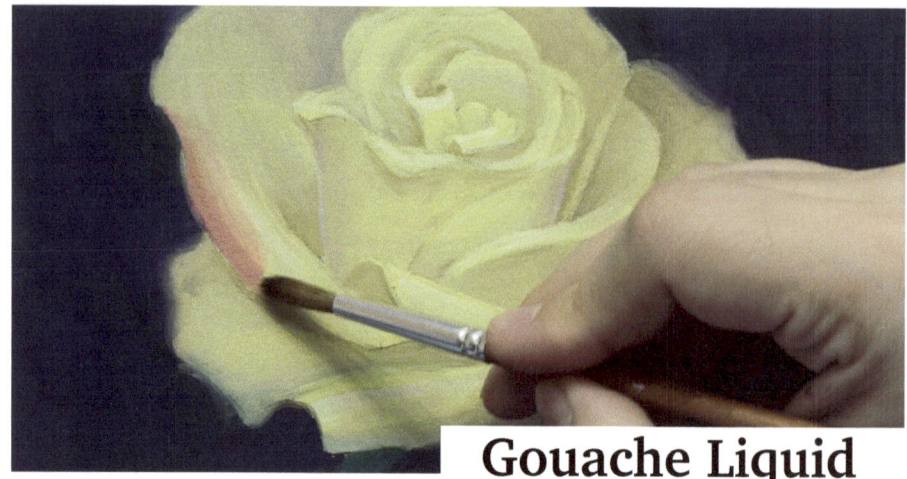

Gouache Liquid

Popularity: 4 from 5

Technique gouache liquid is applied for painting semi-opaque layers and fine detail.

A layer of liquid paint or glaze is used for change shade of ready picture or (it happens much more frequently) piece of picture.

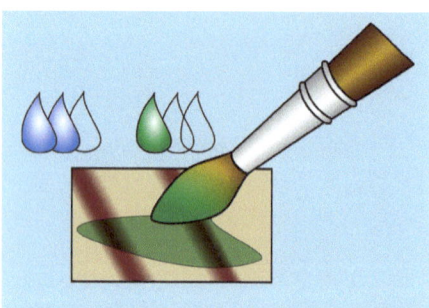

Liquid gouache are applied with thin semi-opaque layers.

Glaze is very popular in all painting techniques: tempera, oil, acrylic, etc.

A using thin paint layer can easy get variety effects and change ratio of colors and tones in picture. A drapery and complex textures will painted very difficult without use a liquid paint.

A liquid gouache (as any liquid paint) can apply with several layers.

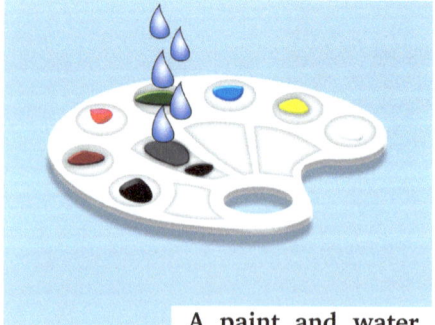

A paint and water are mixed on palette.

A liquid gouache is applied with a semi-opaque layer, and it is not mixed with lowly layers as in used technique wash with paint.

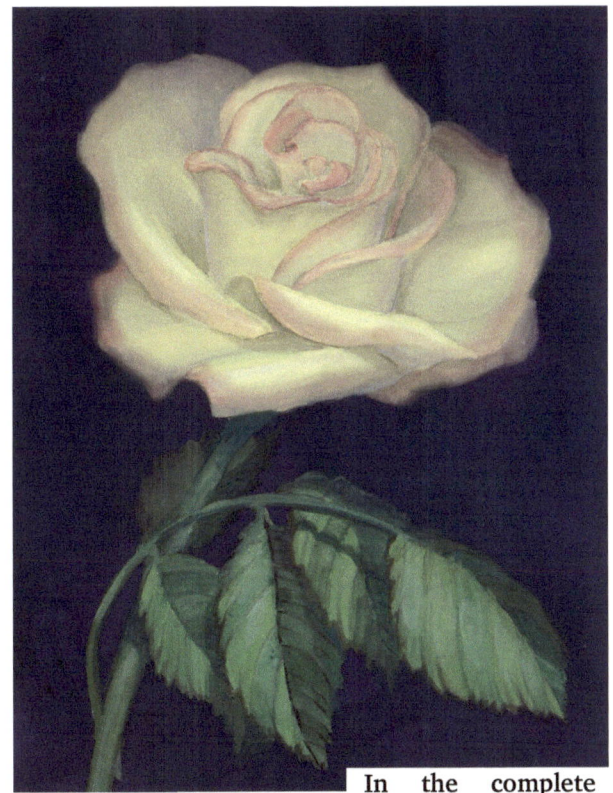

In the complete picture is easy corrected and added details with use gouache liquid. A low layer of picture is not changed.

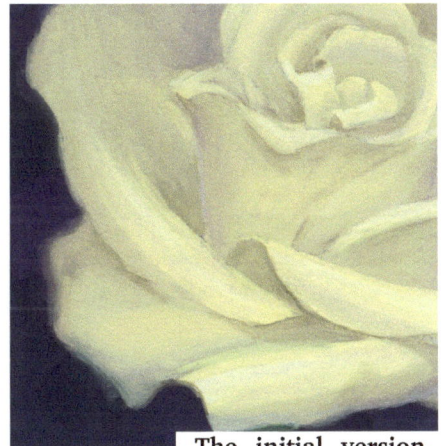

The initial version of picture.

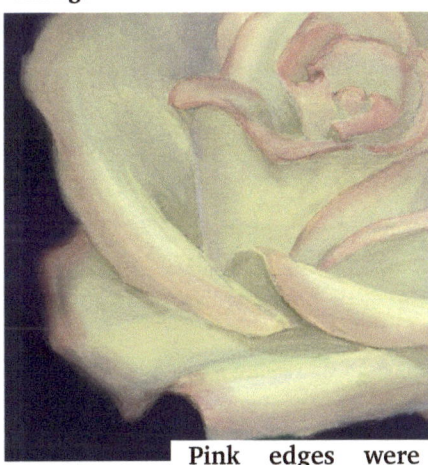

Pink edges were painted with the gouache liquid.

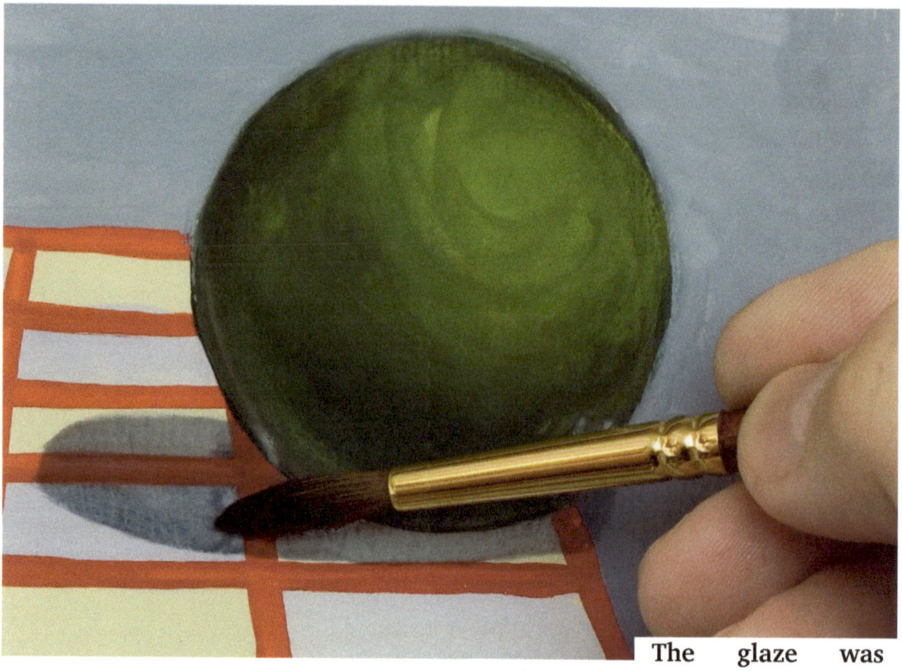

The glaze was applied to one stroke.

Stages of Tehnique

1. A paint and a lot of water is mixed on palette. Liquid of paint is depends on future use.

A very liquid paint - almost water will be used for light lines. They can be after drying used as a drawing for painting.

More thick paint are used for apply semi-opaque layers. They are used for change color or tone of pieces or background of picture. In addition, shadows are made easy and quickly with a liquid paint.

2. The paint is tested on draft.

3. The liquid paint is applied on dry paint surface. For example - dry gradient washing.

This technique is used soft-hair brush: squirrel or soft synthetic. A paint is applied with one or maximum - two brushstrokes.

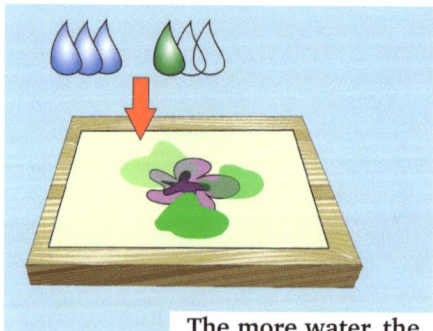

The more water, the more transparent layer.

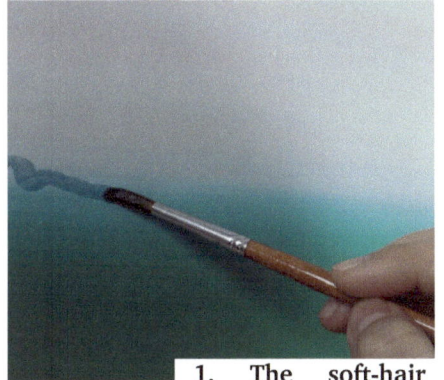

1. The soft-hair brush (squirrel) fits for paint a fine line on gouache background.

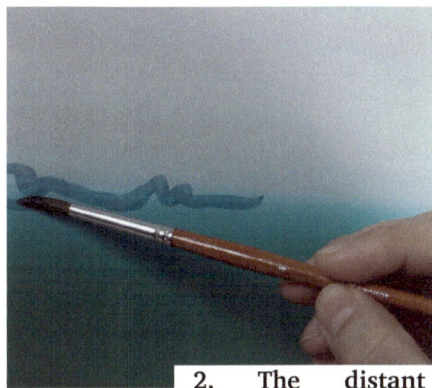

2. The distant forest was painted started from contour.

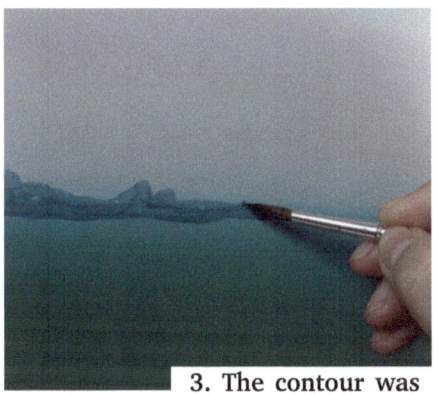

3. The contour was quickly filled, and a paint was not dissolved.

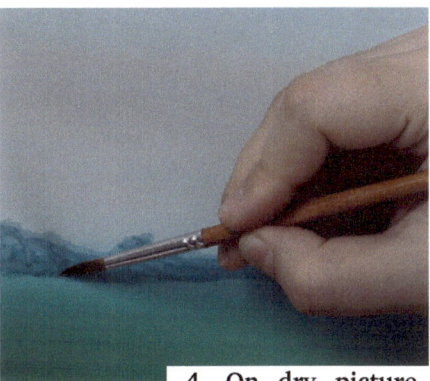

4. On dry picture can be added layer of liquid gouache.

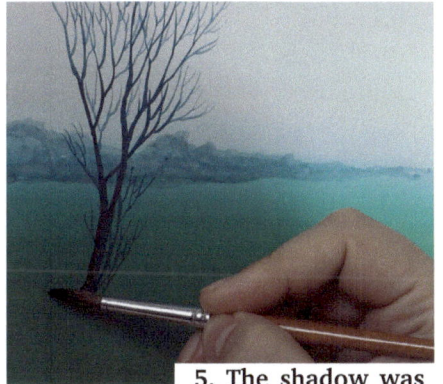

5. The shadow was applied by one brushstroke on shaft of tree and field.

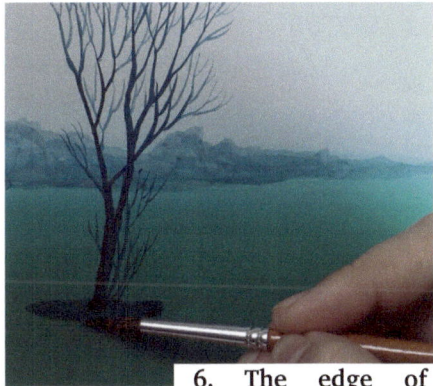

6. The edge of shadow can correct, but quickly or wait, when paint will dry.

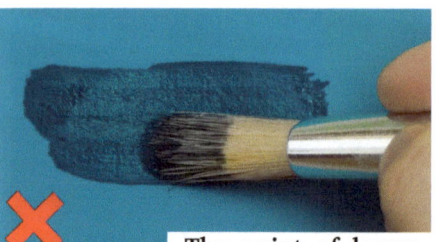

The paint of lower layer was dissolved and in picture strips, because was used a hard-hair brush.

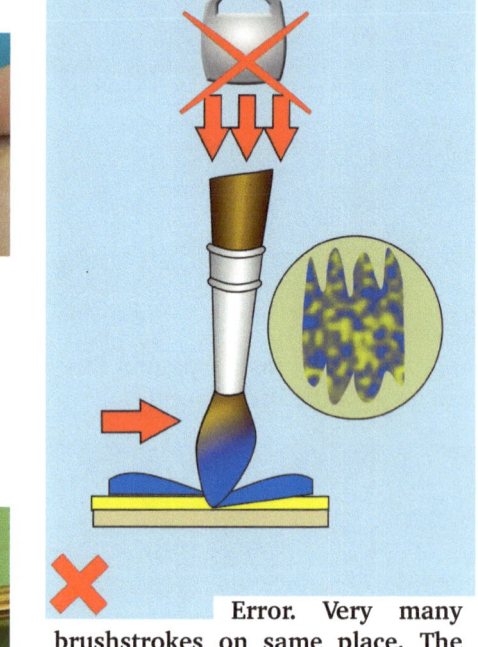

Error. Very many brushstrokes on same place. The result - a wash with paint.

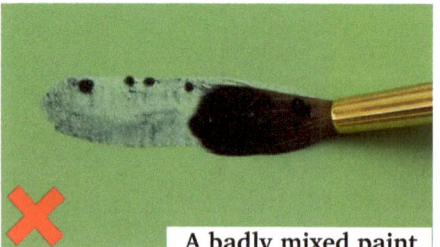

A badly mixed paint includes pallets.

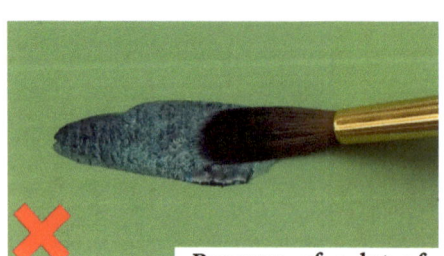

Because of a lot of paint was made puddle. When paint will dry, on its surface will be halo.

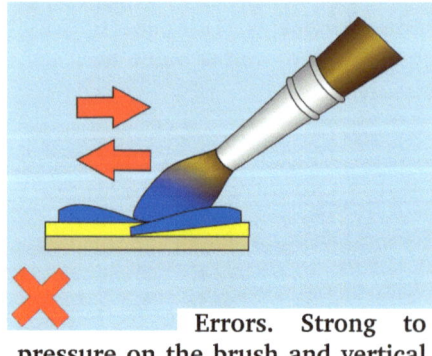

Errors. Strong to pressure on the brush and vertical position of brush. Low layer paint will be dissolved.

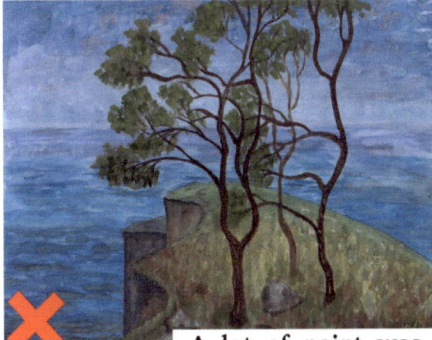

A lot of paint was on a brush. Therefore picture by beginner painter is unsuccessfully looks.

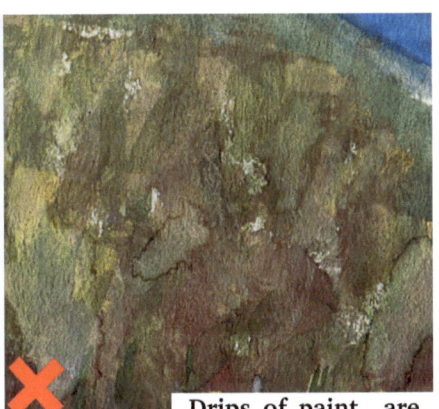

Drips of paint are surrounded dark halo.

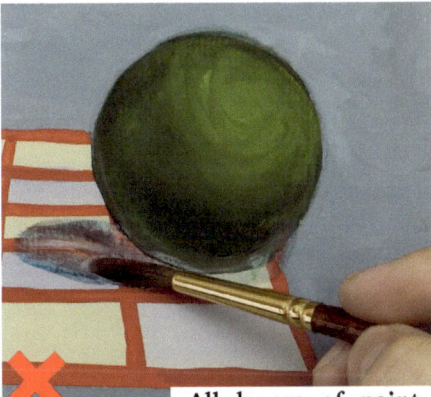

All layers of paint were dissolved and mixed because a long time work and a lot of brushstrokes on same area of picture.

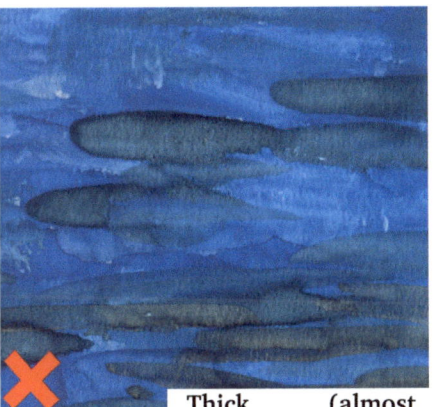

Thick (almost nontransparent) paint was used in this picture.

Exercises

Distant Forest

Take complete gradient washing.

On place of blurred border between color bands: paint with liquid gouache uneven strip like contour of distant forest on sky background.

Paint a bottom border of the forest.

Fill with a liquid paint the contour of forest. On a sheet should not be a lot of paint. Otherwise in the contour of forest will be puddles.

Make Shadow

Take your a ready gouache picture of house or tree on gradient washing. Paint a shadow of their with a gouache liquid.

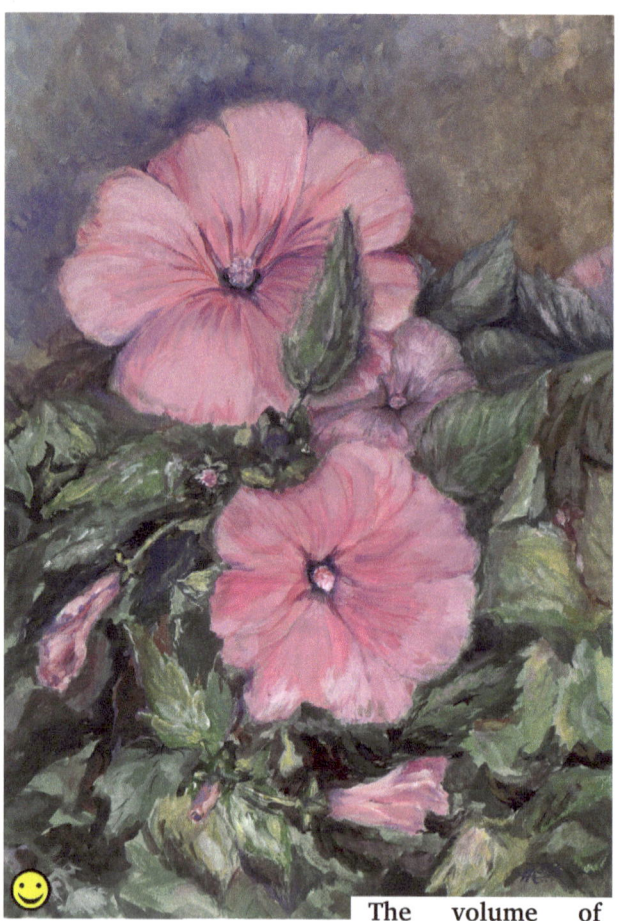

The volume of flowers was painted to several layers.

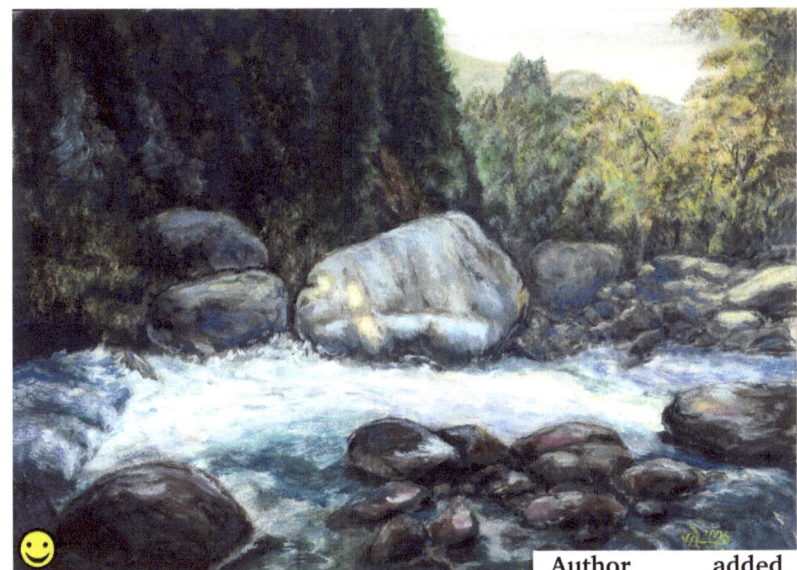

Author added shades of pink and blue with gouache liquid.

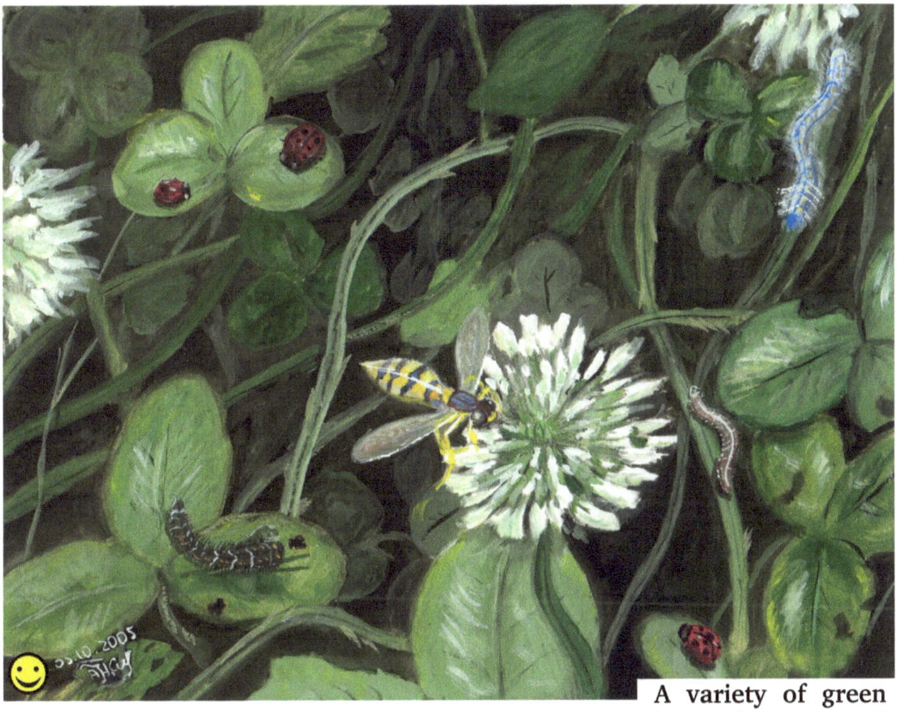

A variety of green shades was obtained to several layers of liquid paint.

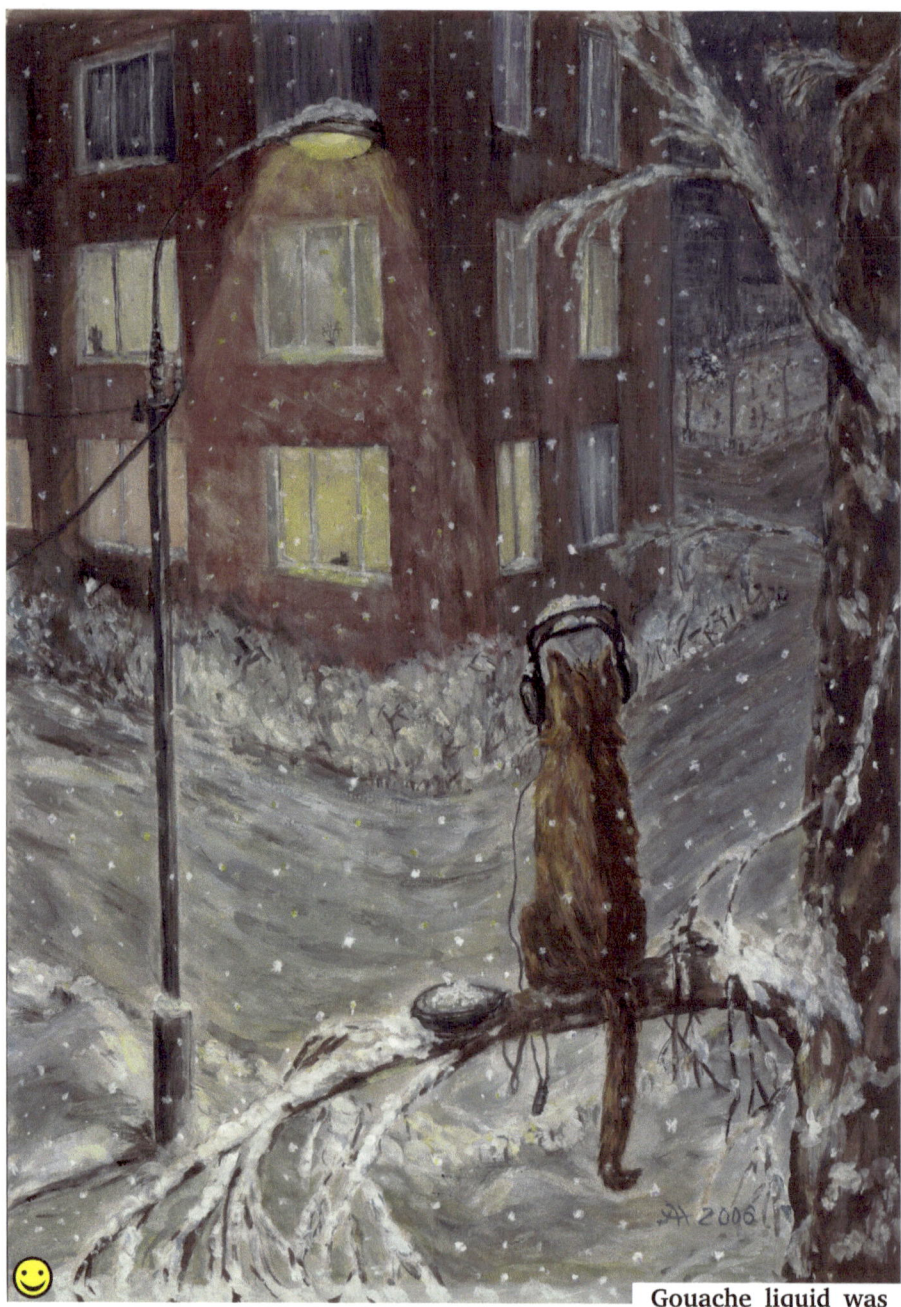

Gouache liquid was used in many places of picture. For example: on distant houses were overlaid layer of liquid white paint.

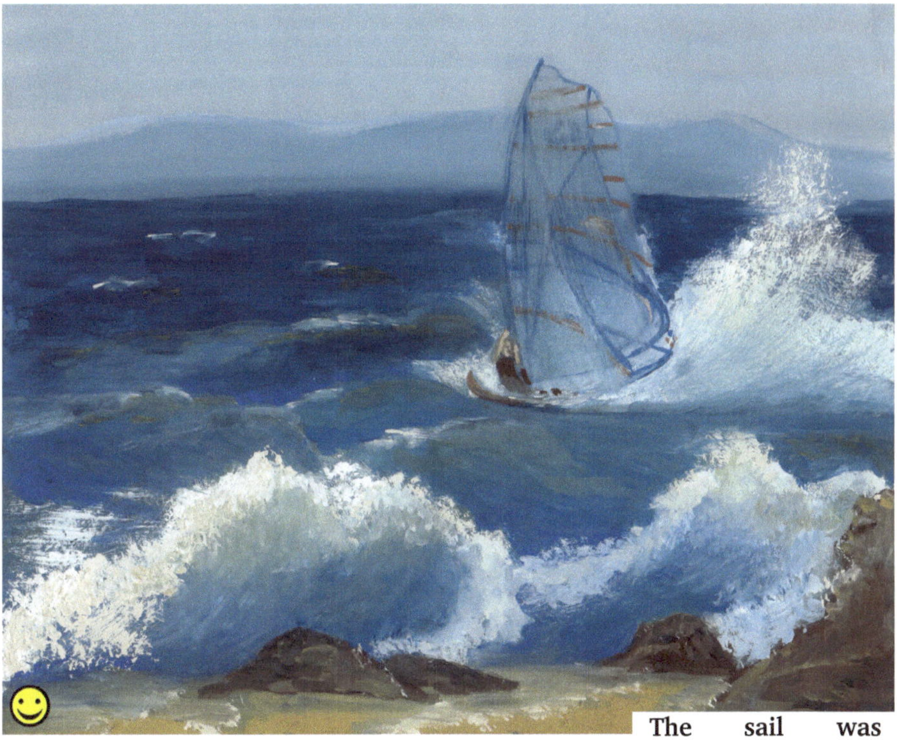

![A gouache painting of a sailboat on stormy seas with crashing waves and mountains in the background](image)

The sail was painted with a light and liquid layer of paint.

Helpful Tips

A color mixtures with a ocher and white after drying will much lighter. Do not use these colors to mixtures for paint shadows.

If a layer of gouache liquid don't fit, should wait complete drying. After drying can apply new layer.

Compatibility with Other Techniques

Gouache liquid can be used together with any techniques.

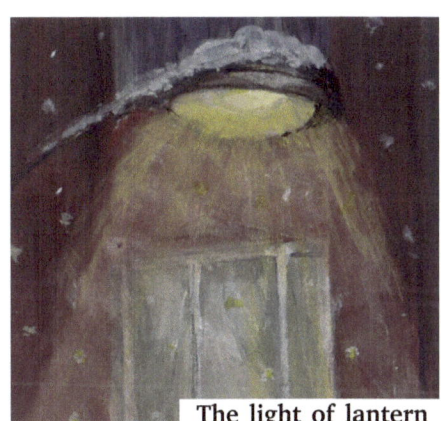

The light of lantern was painted to several layers.
First: a glaze was applied white gouache. After this was applied gold ocher.

Path Between Hills

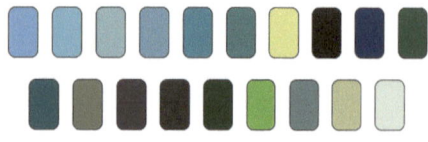

Color mixtures

Used techniques: gradient washing, gouache liquid, fine lines, opaque layers, softening edges, uniform staining.

The picture painted at sheet 30x21 cm (12x8,25 in). With self-painting can take anywhere from 2 to 3 hours.

1. The gradient washing will painted without detailed drawing.

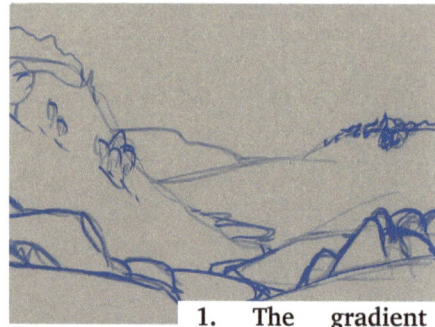

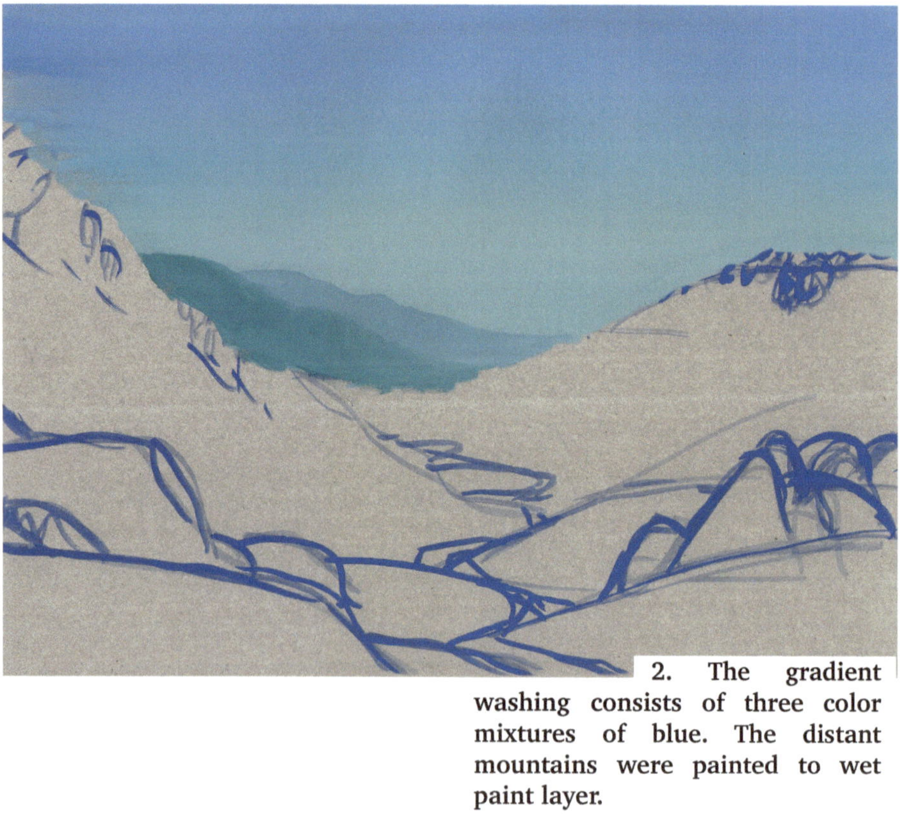

2. The gradient washing consists of three color mixtures of blue. The distant mountains were painted to wet paint layer.

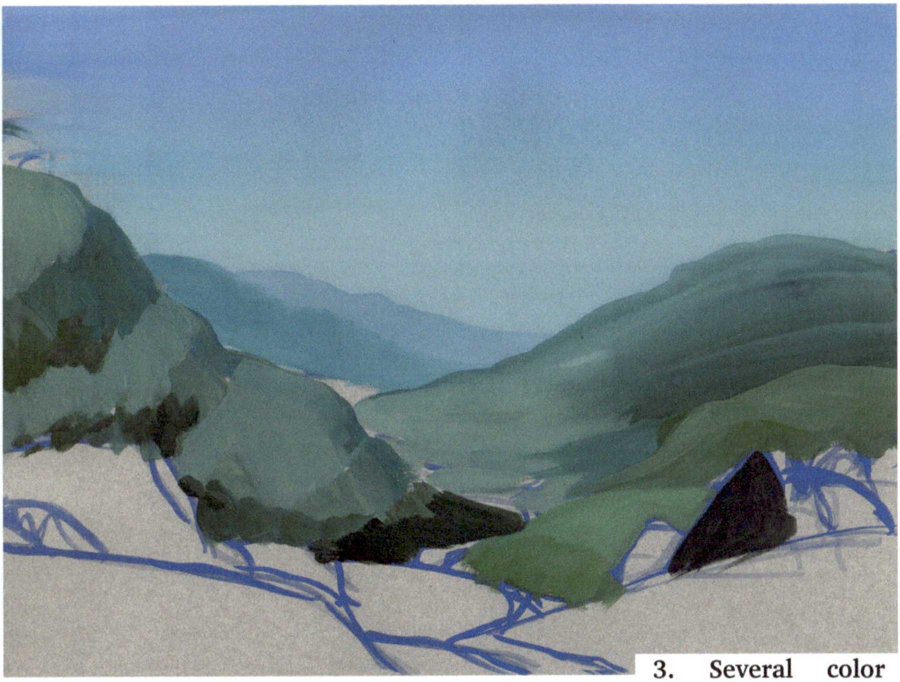

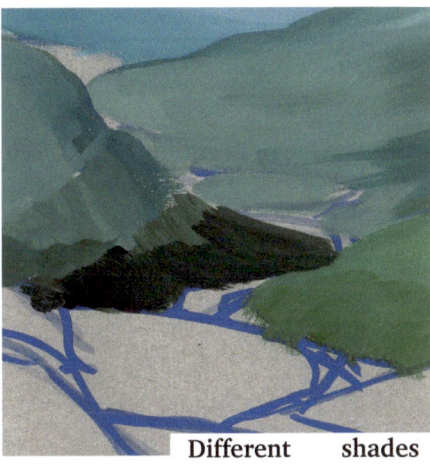

3. Several color mixtures of green were mixed on a palette in advance. Lightings were painted to different color mixtures.

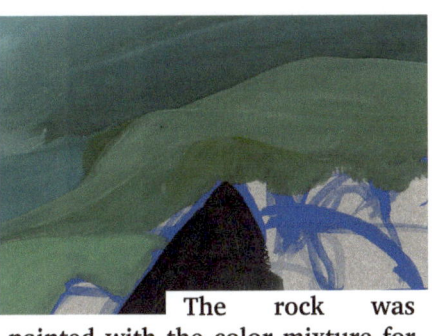

The rock was painted with the color mixture for shadows.

Different shades added picturesqueness.

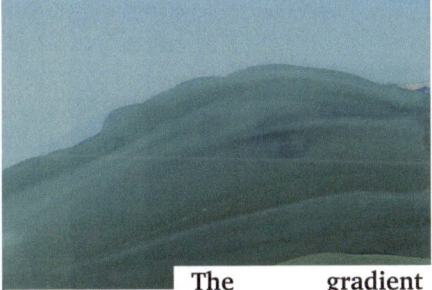

The gradient washing of hill was not completely smoothed.

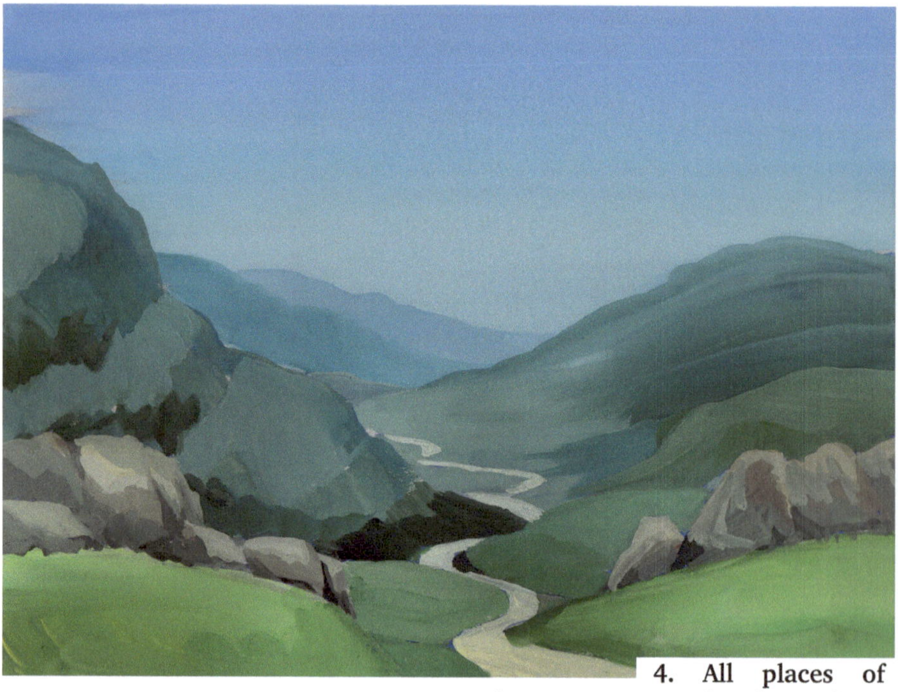

4. All places of picture were painted without details.

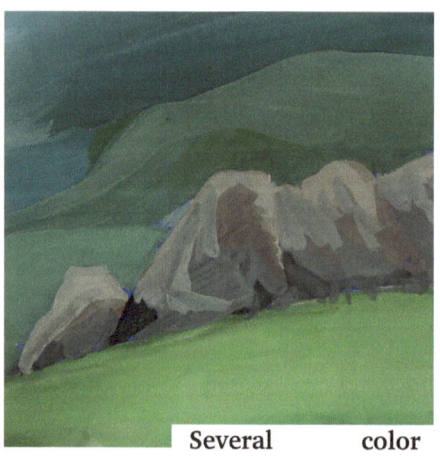

Several color mixtures for rocks were mixed on a palette in advance. The penumbra on rocks was painted with gouache liquid

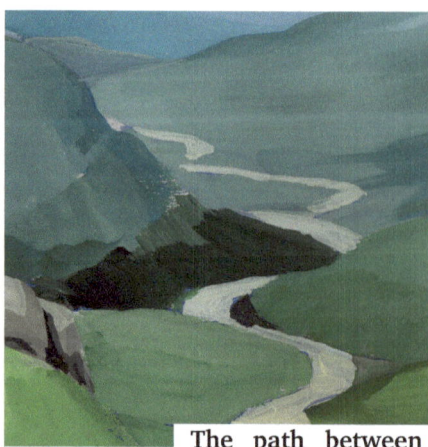

The path between hills is completely painted.

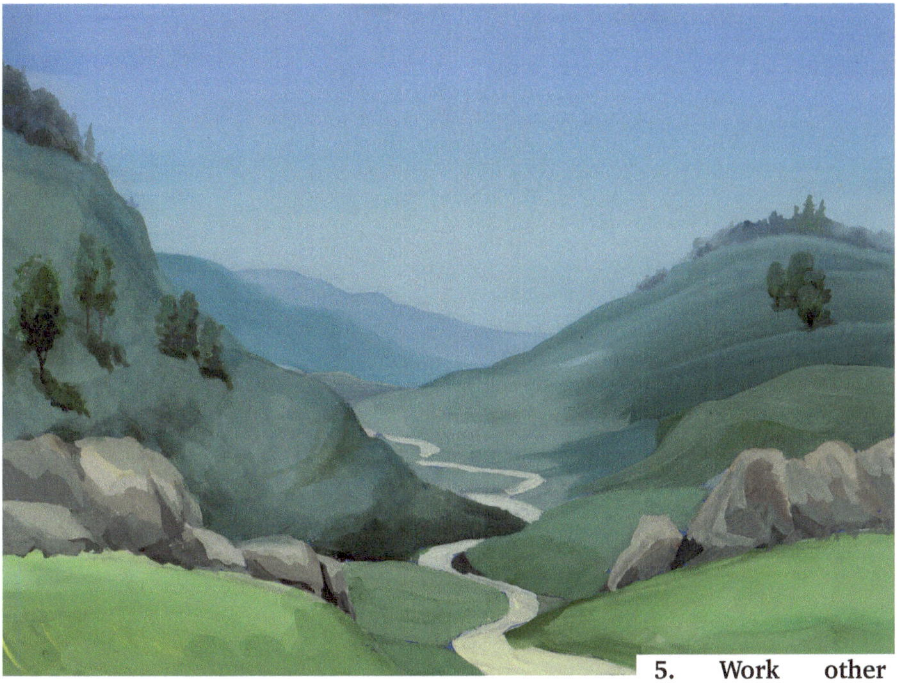

5. Work other details starts.

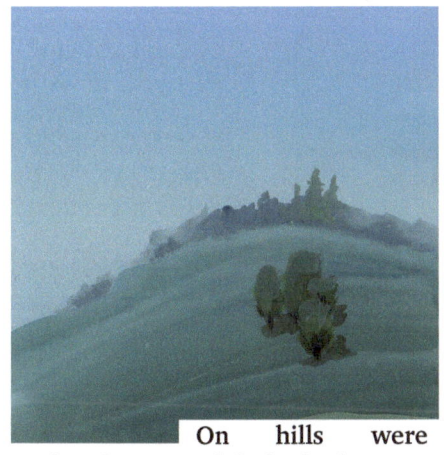

On hills were painted trees and their shadows.

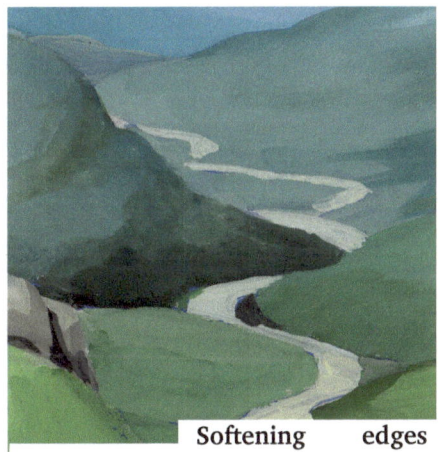

Softening edges gives more volume.

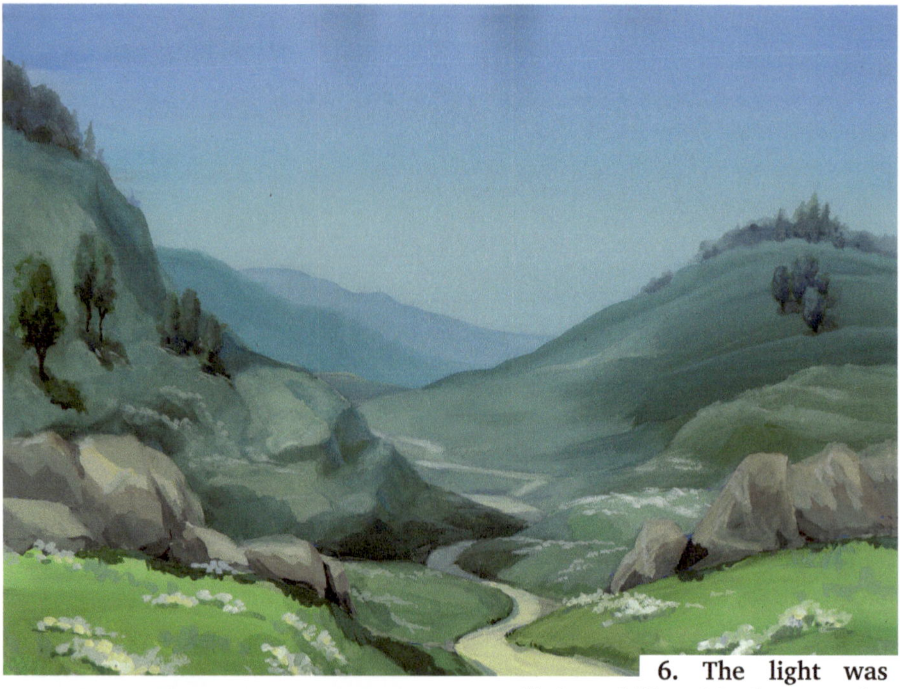

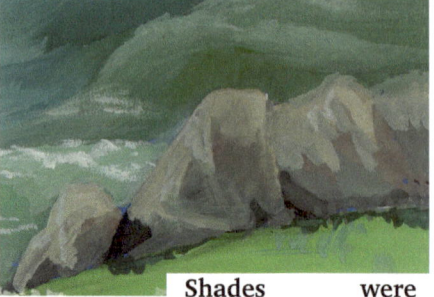

6. The light was applied on hills with the gouache liquid.

Shades were applied on rocks with the gouache liquid.

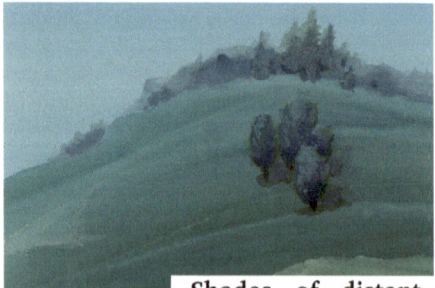

Shades of distant forest and trees were added with the gouache liquid.

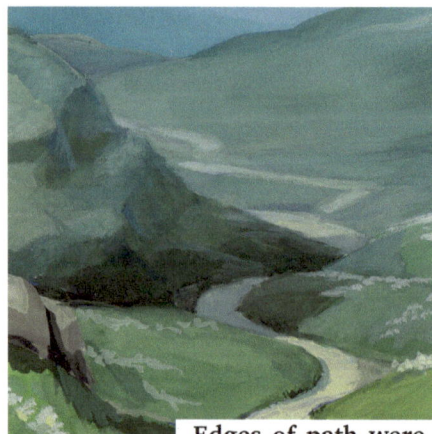

Edges of path were softened. The shadow on path was painted with the opaque layer. The flowers were painted to a several shades of opaque layers.

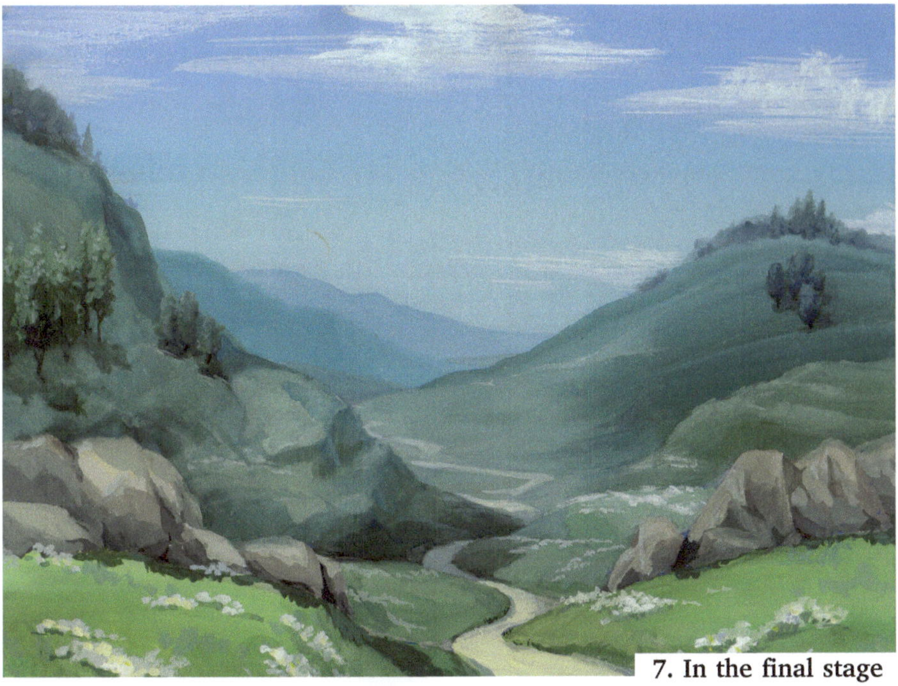

7. In the final stage details were complete and clouds were painted with gouache liquid.

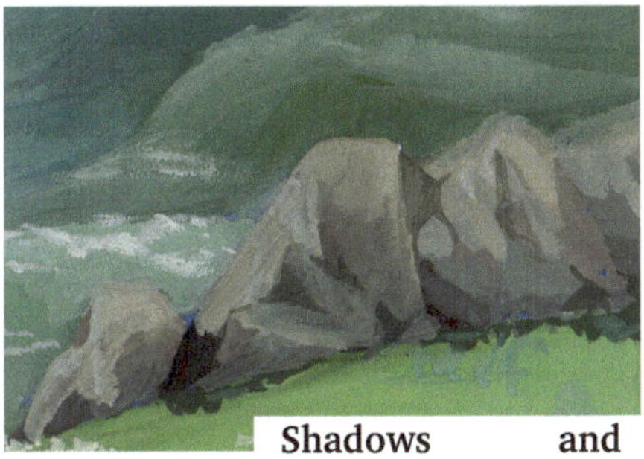

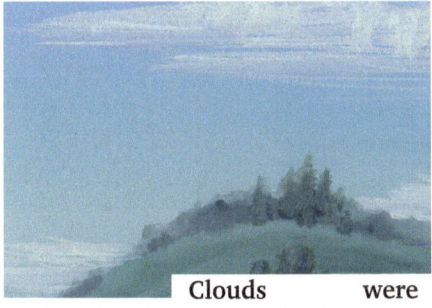

Shadows and cracks were applied on rocks.

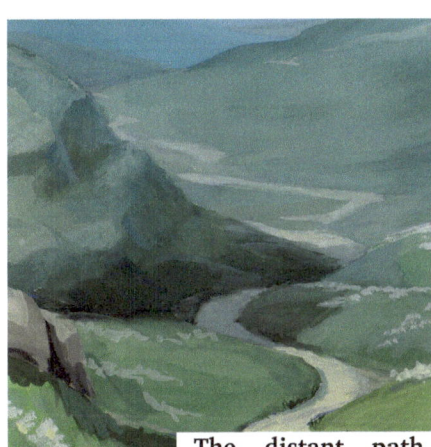

The distant path was added on sheet.

Clouds were painted with the gouache liquid.

Frosty Afternoon

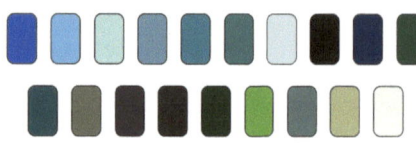

Used techniques: gradient washing, gouache liquid, fine lines, opaque layers, softening edges.

The picture painted at sheet 30x37 cm (12x14,5 in). With self-painting can take anywhere from 3 to 4 hours.

1. The gradient wash will painted to three color mixtures for sky and three color mixtures for snow. Hills will painted to wet paint.

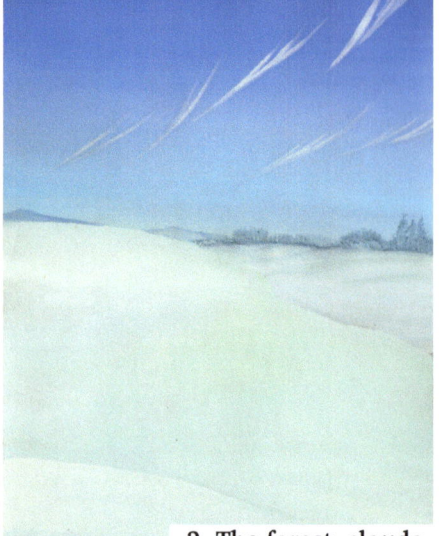

2. The forest, clouds and hills were painted at one time.

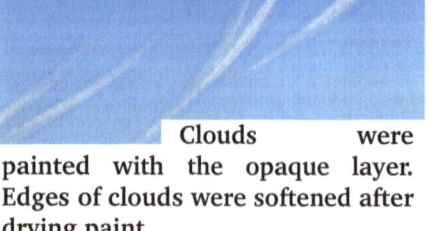

Clouds were painted with the opaque layer. Edges of clouds were softened after drying paint.

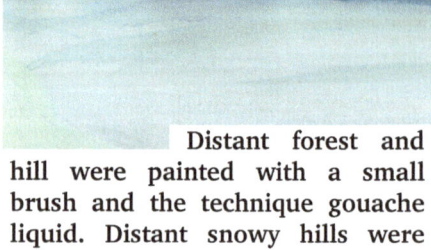

Distant forest and hill were painted with a small brush and the technique gouache liquid. Distant snowy hills were painted with gouache liquid too.

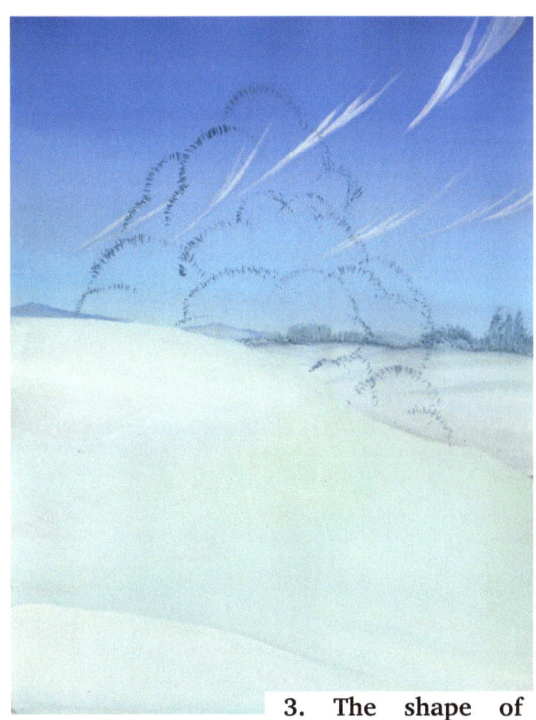

3. The shape of future tree is marked with tips of branches.

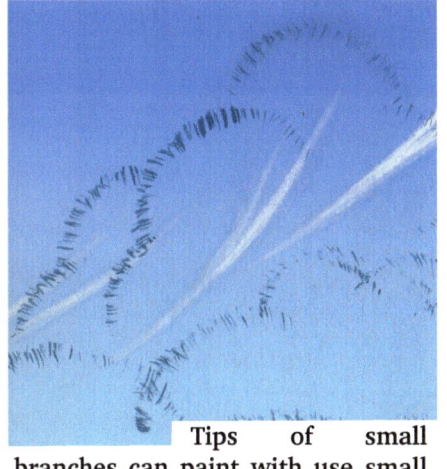

Tips of small branches can paint with use small brush or dry brushwork.

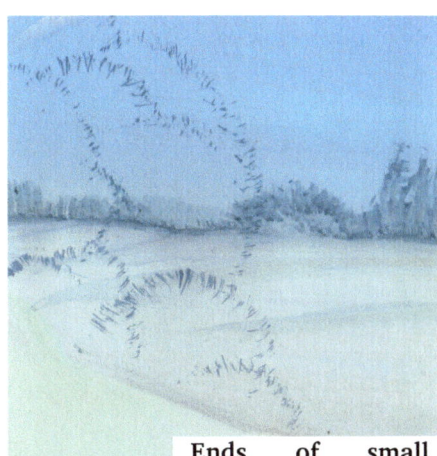

Ends of small branches that are outer boundary of tree.

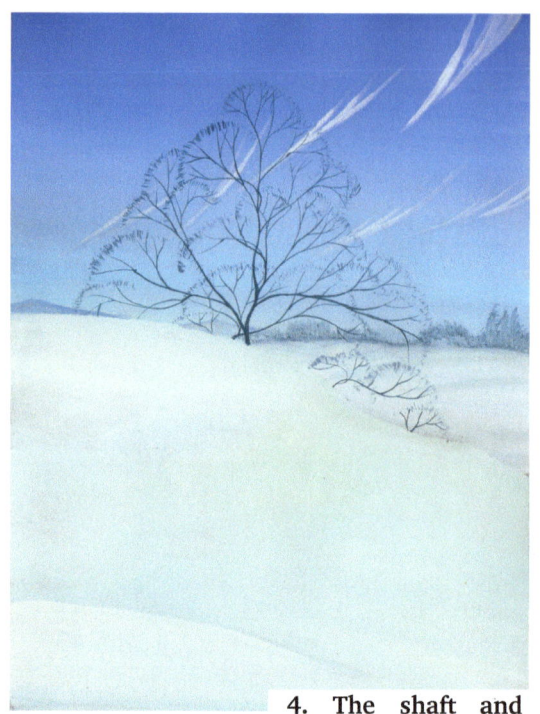

4. The shaft and main branches of tree were painted to technique fine line. A color mixture should be light-gray.

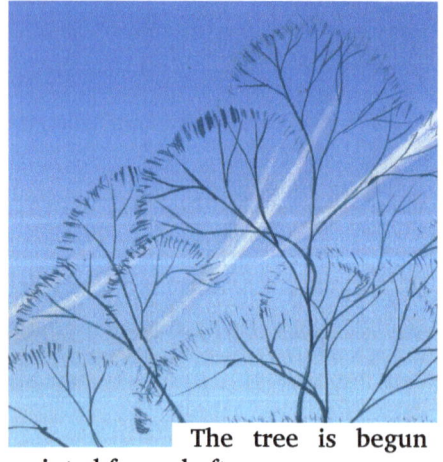

The tree is begun painted from shaft.

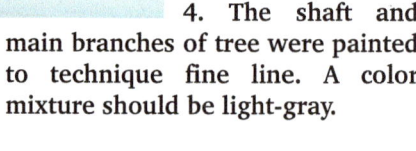

On brush should be liquid paint.

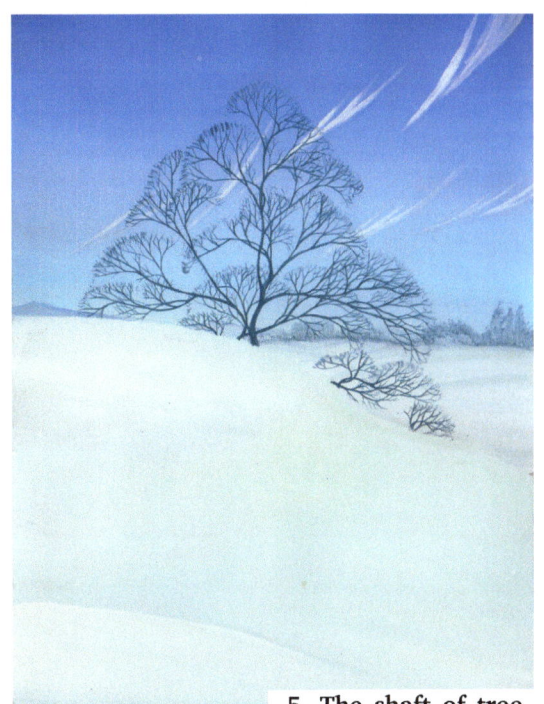

5. The shaft of tree and new branches were painted color mixture darker, than the previous stage.

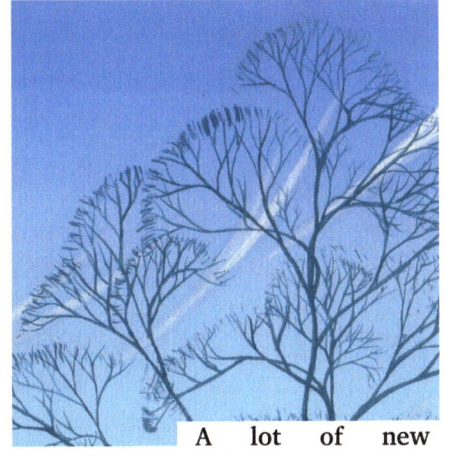

A lot of new branches were painted with a dark-gray color mixture.

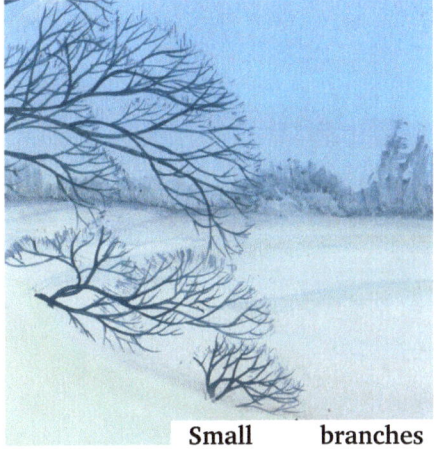

Small branches must paint shipshape.

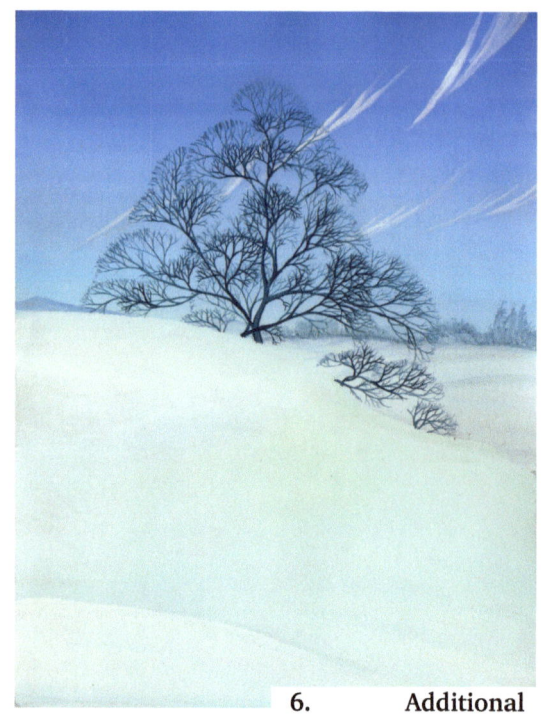

6. Additional branches were painted color mixture darker than the previous stage.

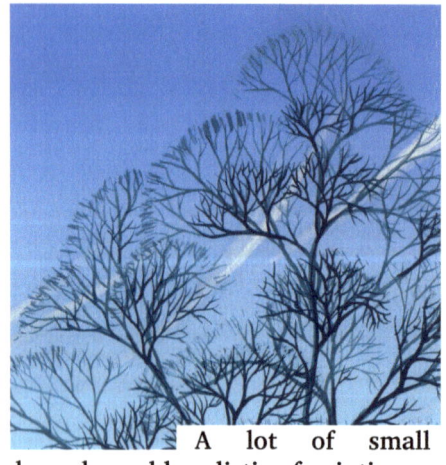

A lot of small branches add realistic of painting.

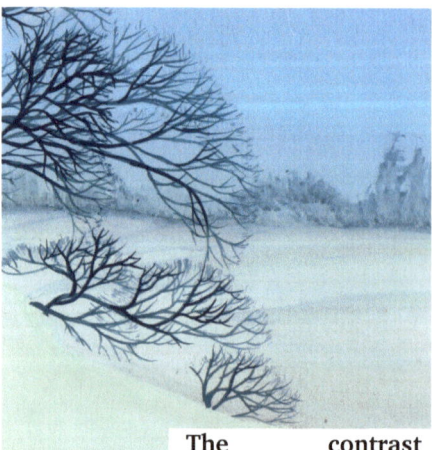

The contrast picture: dark branches on the snow.

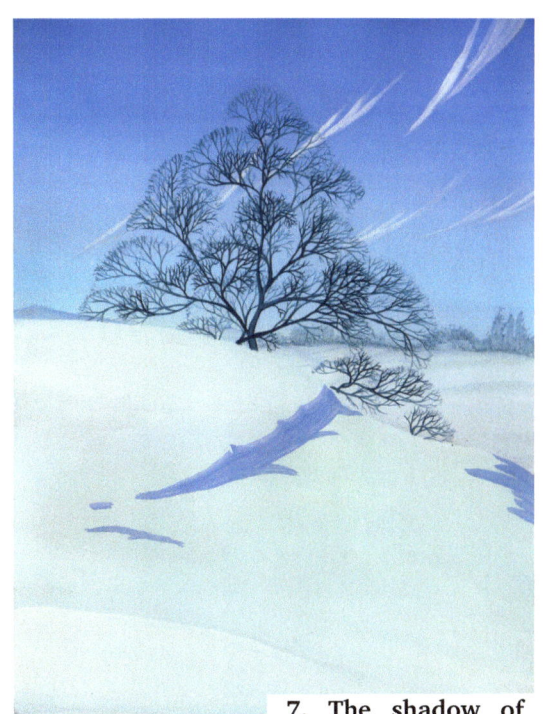

7. The shadow of snowdrift was painted with a blue liquid paint

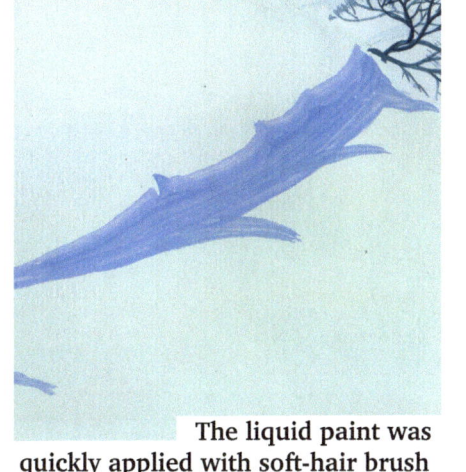

The liquid paint was quickly applied with soft-hair brush

The blue spot will be a shadow of the snowdrift.

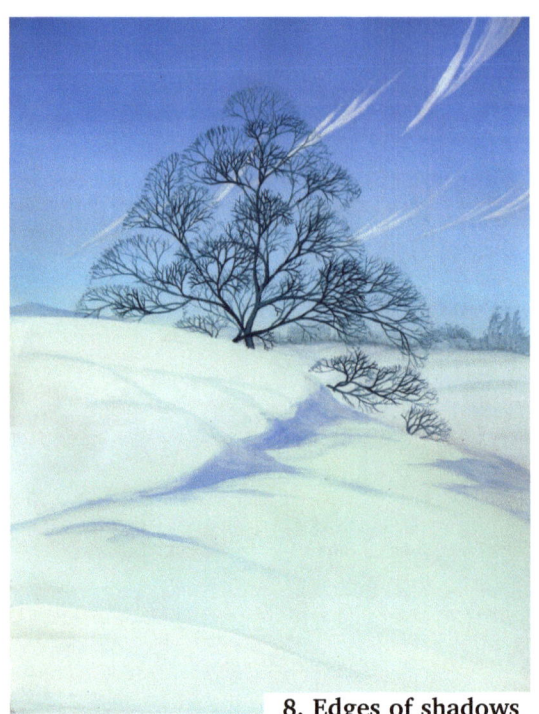

8. Edges of shadows of snowdrift were softened.

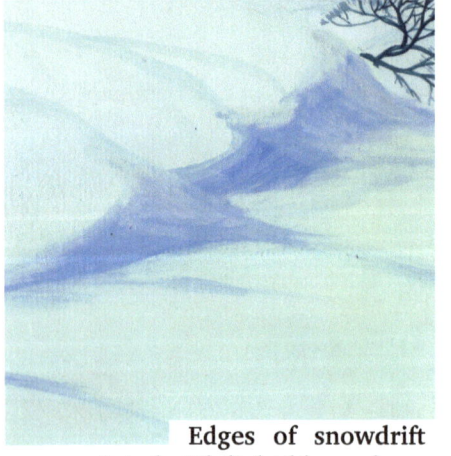

Edges of snowdrift were painted with light-blue color.

The blue spot has become shadow of snowdrift.

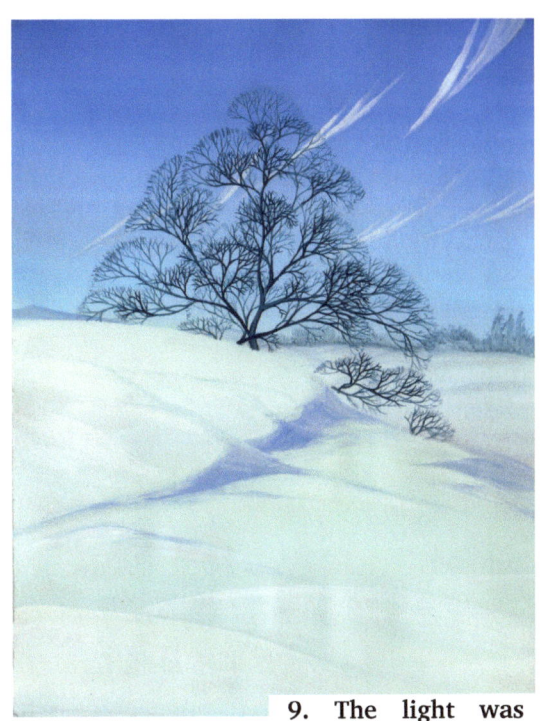

9. The light was applied on snowdrift with light color mixture with adding ocher.

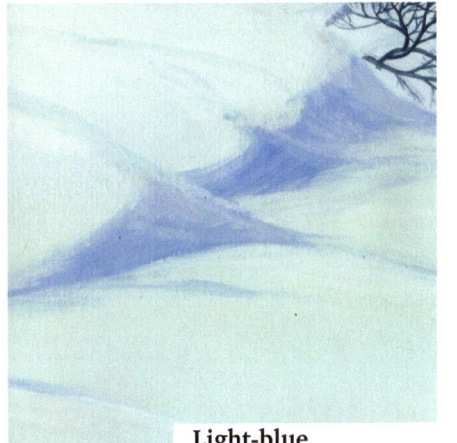

Light-blue brushstrokes were overpaint with liquid white gouache.

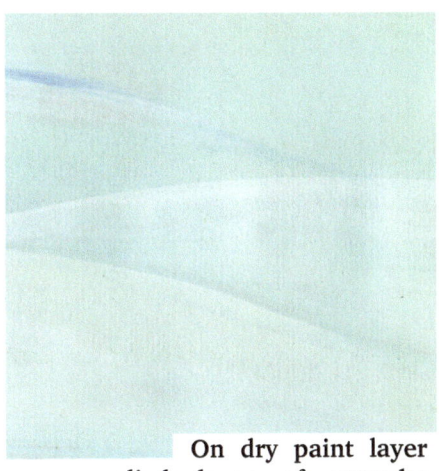

On dry paint layer was applied layer of gouache liquid.

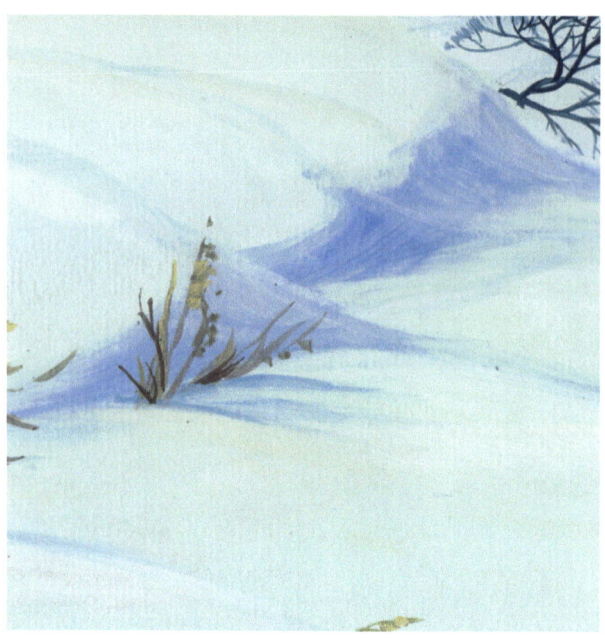

Dry grasses were painted with a liquid paint several shades of brown. The light was applied on grass with the opaque layer.

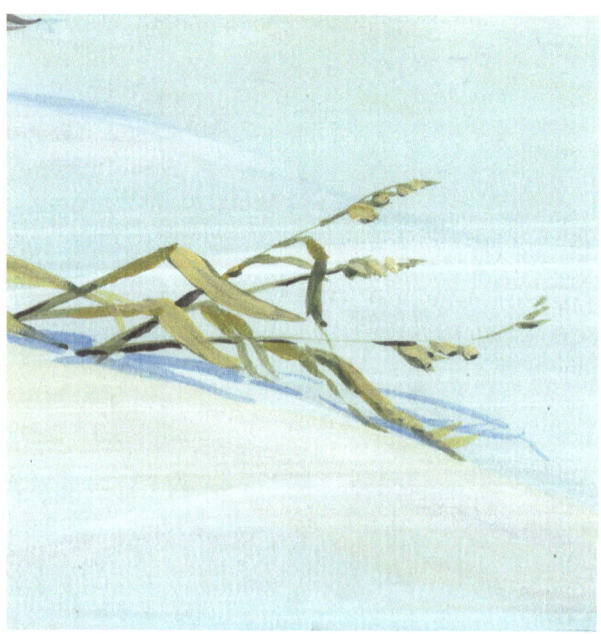

On snow were painted shadows and yellowish reflections of grass.

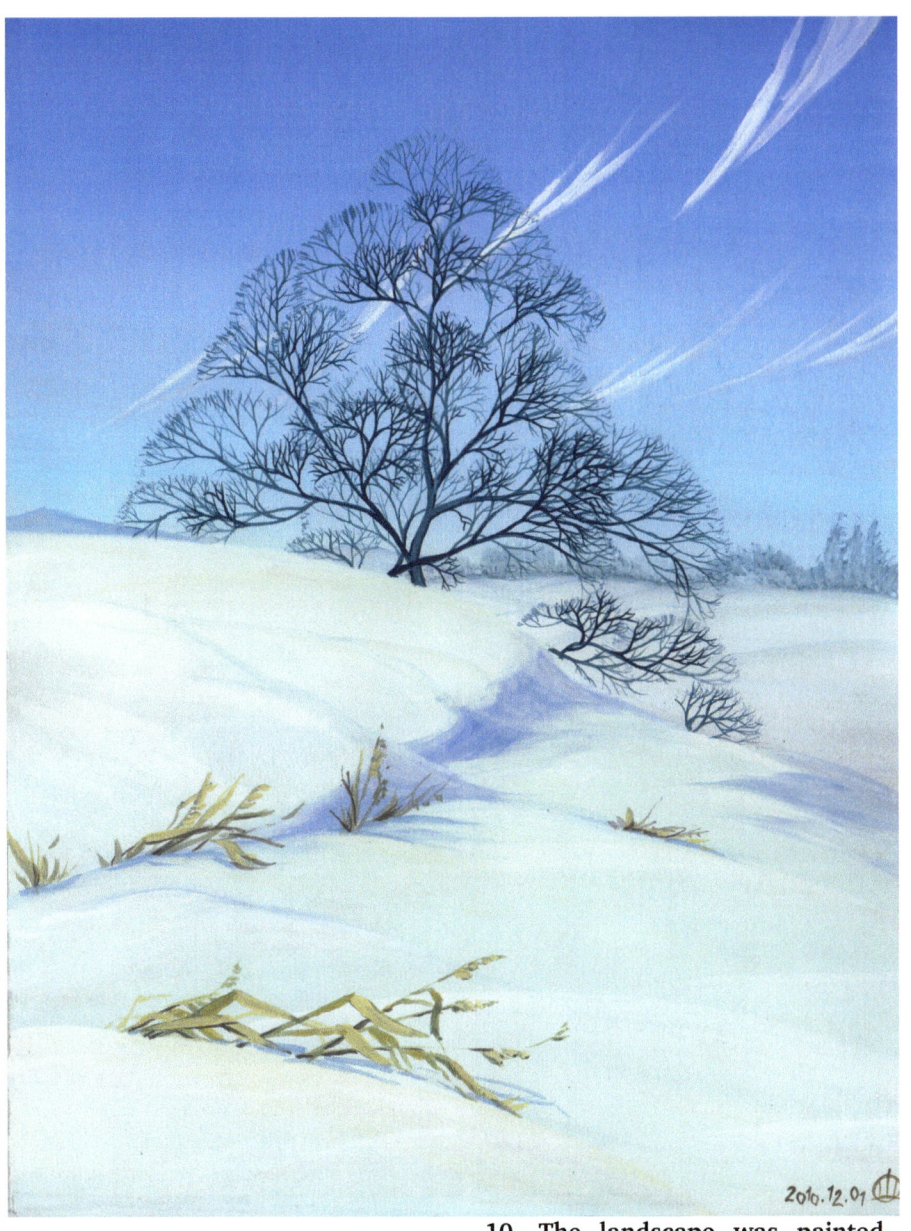

10. The landscape was painted after walk in frost - 30 C (- 22 F)

Summary of All The Volumes Techniques Gouache Painting

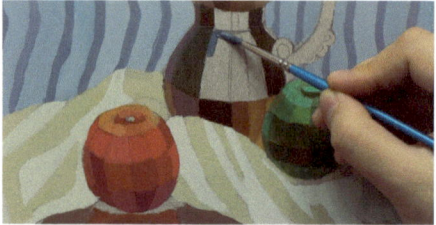

Uniform Staining
Uniform Staining is used for overlaying support with uniformly and thin paints layer.

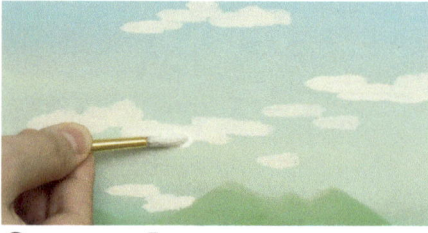

Opaque Layers
Opaque Layers are used to hide a bottom layers.

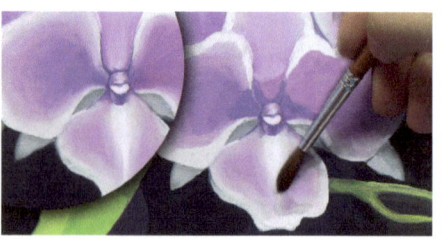

Softening Edges
Softening edges use for make gradient between brushstrokes.

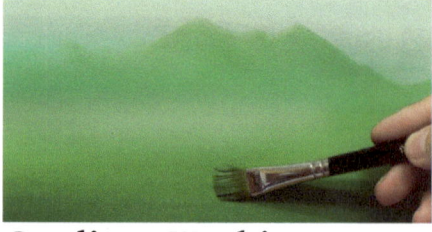

Gradient Washing
Color gradient to large area is making with technique Gradient Washing.

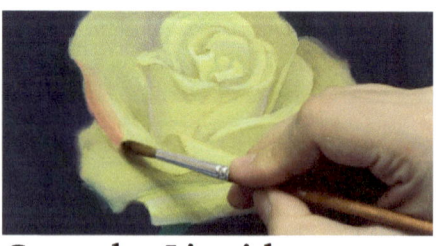

Gouache Liquid
Technique Gouache Liquid is applied for painting semi-opaque layers and fine detail.

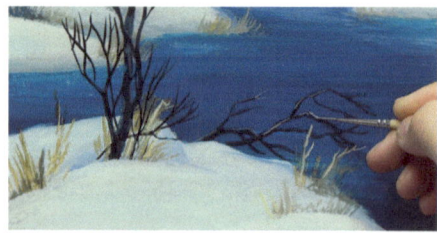

Fine Lines
This technique used for painting fine lines with gouache.

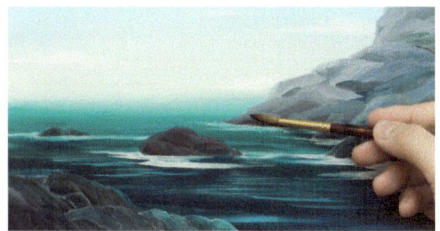

Liquid Guache First Layer

The used transparent layer with very liquid gouache.

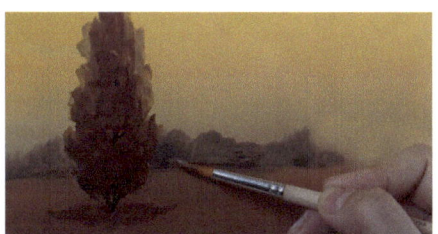

Wash with Paint

Mix paints on to canvas without palette.

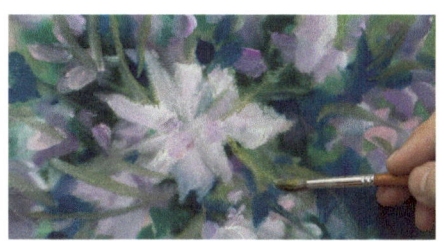

Gouache-to-Wet

This is technique for applying brushstrokes on wet background.

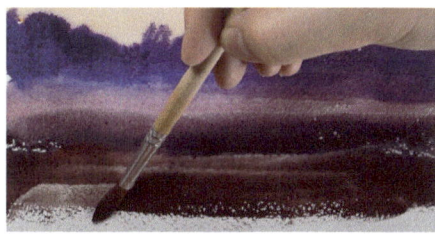

Wash with Water

The use blending to dry paint of upper and low layers.

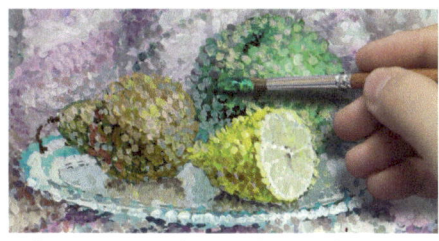

Sharp and Multicolor Brushstrokes

Brushstrokes how mosaic. Every brushstroke separately, don't mixed with others.

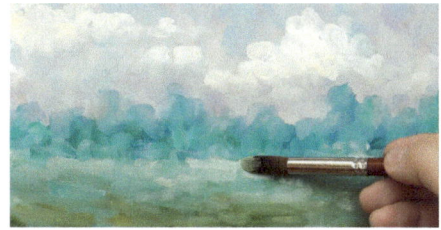

Blurred Brushstrokes

The blurred brushstrokes are applied on dry background.

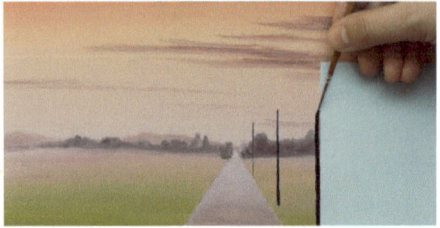

Stencils and Masks

Stencil and mask used for corrected picture and adding elements.

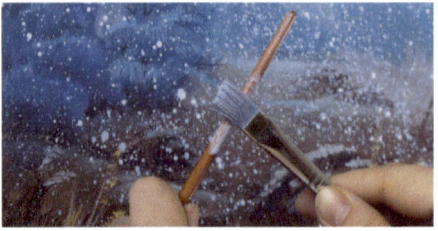

Spattering

This can making a lot of small specks at picture.

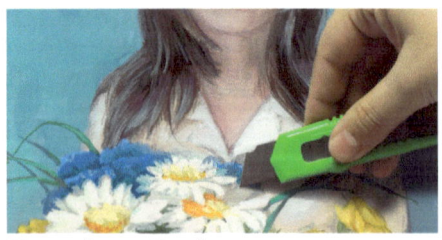

Erasing Paint

If correction with other techniques can not used, then paint is erased.

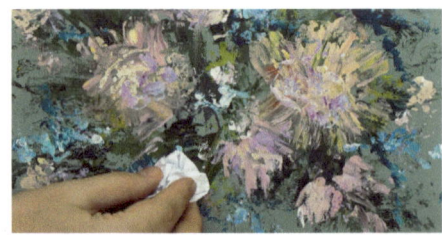

Stamping

This technique is used for fill a area with same prints. Stamp can used as brush.

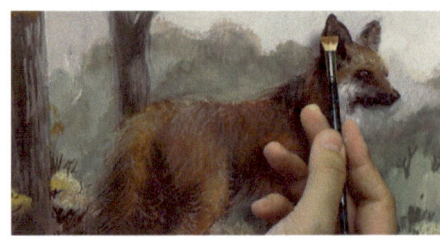

Dray Brushwork

The dry brushwork used for create much thin stripes painted in the same direction.

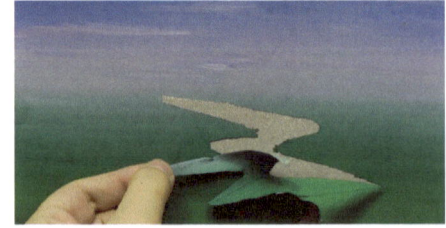

Masking Support

The masking is used to isolate area of support from paint.